HIDDEN STORIES OF THE CHILDHOOD OF JESUS

Volume One

By Glenn Kimball

BF Publishing, Houston, Texas

HIDDEN STORIES OF THE CHILDHOOD OF JESUS

THE COVER: Designed in part by Dave Stirland. The cover
represents the prophetic Star of Bethlehem as it likely appeared
to the Magi who came to visit the infant Jesus.

ACKNOWLEDGMENTS

The inspiration of friends has become increasingly important to me. I would like to thank my friend, David Stirland and his wife, Beth Ann (Sunny), who both contributed to the momentum of this book and to its contents. I would like to thank my brother, Tom, for the idea and my sisters, Mary, Page, and Lynda, for their help with the manuscript. I would also like to thank Steve Bowers and Keith Gurr for their encouragement. I couldn't forget my children, Dayna, Chase, Kellianne, and David, who are my personal life. A special thank you to Etta, who spent time with me when I needed a real friend.

Also, a special thanks to my parents, Esther and Elden, who believed in me when I needed it most and who will always be the reason for any success in my life.

Glenn Kimball

Dedication

To my very best friend,
Duffy Hunter, who
always told me the
eagles would fly again.

Hidden

Treasure

Series

Volume One

For more information about the "Hidden Treasure Series," visit us at **www.ancientmanuscripts.com**. This site will have a variety of interactive services and the latest updates on future volumes. Come and experience the sweet messages of Jesus.

http://www.ancientmanuscripts.com

ℋidden 𝒯reasure 𝒮eries

Volume One

INTRODUCTION

The Hidden Treasure series is designed to be like a tour through Christianity for the common man. We will stop at many newly discovered junctures of history and then return you to your own faith all the better for the insight.

It is different from any other history of Jesus that has ever been written before in several ways. We must remember that the traditional histories of Jesus have either been written by the faithless scholars, who didn't believe in Jesus, or by churchmen who have felt the pressure from their own churches to conform. The word "heresy" was artificially manufactured to protect the churches from Christian discovery without church permission. There haven't been histories written by believers who stood neutrally between the churches and who have defied the scholars in their skepticism. The sword of discovery will be used against the very same faithless scholars who have tried to use that sword of discovery in an attempt to discredit the story of Jesus. In their minds, the strange story they have uncovered didn't match with modern Christian dogma; they are both right and wrong in that assumption. The newly discovered stories are strange indeed; however, they vindicate Jesus more clearly now than before.

Once we dispose of these defensive perspectives, there emerges a wealth of additional information about the life of Jesus and his impact on the whole world that has either been isolated and/or discredited without justification. The additional records weren't false, they just had individual weaknesses that have been exploited by both sides for one reason or another. The whole story resurrects the life of Jesus again in our minds. Jesus re-emerges as the most influential entity the world has ever known, not only spiritually, but politically as well. Jesus deeply affected countless cultures and governments, though Jesus has never fully been given the credit.

The seal of finality on the Bible is now broken, and extra-biblical material floods in to fill in the gaping holes in the story of Christianity. The sheer volume of Jesus' own words, and those of his apostles found in modern times, dwarf the biblical recitation.

Each of the books in this series will take a part of the story that has never been integrated into the big picture and will tie it into the new emerging story of Jesus. Therefore, it will be helpful to read the series from book one on in order to be able to pick up the players and place them in context as the story progresses. There are some very new names of characters in Christian history that stood alongside Jesus in his time. Some of the supposed villains were not such bad guys after all.

The series is designed to give the common reader an historical education of Christianity in a way that he can understand. When you read this history, you might say, "I heard something about that before somewhere, but I didn't realize how important it was." You will not have to purchase the huge anthologies, or find the rare documents. If you do, however, much of the complexity of those writings will make more sense. The series will sequence events and personalities so that the picture of Jesus will be brought into focus. You will be astounded at how many of the obscure passages in the Bible itself suddenly make sense.

There are weaknesses in each of the extra-biblical texts. However, when these texts are brought together in one place, and placed into historical context, the peripheral historical evidence solidifies many of those weaknesses. The critics of the story have long used the "divide and conquer" approach to discredit any additional story of Jesus. However, that strategy will prove lacking in this history. We will use many different sources to verify those same events without fear, instead of being limited to the Bible.

This series is not intended to proselyte. We encourage the reader to return to his own individual faith with renewed enthusiasm, but with a better understanding of the history. The reader should not fear a history that, in the end, vindicates Jesus. People feared Jesus before He was born, and they continue to fear the total picture of His history today. It is time we replace the fear with the real spirit of the message of Jesus. It is time that the common man possess the secrets of Christianity and decide for himself, instead of being told that the rest of the story isn't important, or is a mystery that he is not intelligent enough to understand.

There is enough material to write a hundred books in the series. However, we have attempted to be both patient and aggressive in revealing the additional discoveries. You will find that the story doesn't lag at all. It reads like banner headlines from a newspaper by design. Each of the books in the series will focus on one perspective in history. The series may not be in chronological order, but each book is sequenced for a very good reason. The order of presentation builds a foundation for understanding the importance of each of the subsequent events. We have begun with some spectacularly new basic discoveries, like the childhood stories of Jesus, that will illustrate the significance of the hidden documents. The later books in the series will take increasingly more complex discoveries and graft them to that foundation.

The first step is to understand that the world possesses much more about the life of Jesus than we have been spoon-fed. You will be astonished at how much there is. For example, Jesus was performing miracles from the time He was a Baby, and His life's history extends outside of Judea and integrates into many very different cultures and countries during his lifetime. Hang on to your seat—you're in for the ride of your life! It may broaden your vision more than you anticipate.

Table of Contents

Section One

HIDDEN STORIES OF THE CHILDHOOD OF JESUS

Section Two

STORY OF THE
HOLY FAMILY

Chapter 11

Chapter 12

Chapter 1

HIDDEN STORIES OF THE CHILDHOOD OF JESUS

OVERVIEW

There are three very separate parts to this book. Each are designed to be a different kind of introduction to the enormous field of extra-biblical Christian documents, especially as they relate to the childhood of Jesus. The first is intended to both orient the reader to the nature of ancient Christian documents, which may shake loose the adventurous spirit of discovery from any preconceived notions, and to answer the question, "Why don't we know anything about the childhood of Jesus?"

The second part of the book contains the actual ancient stories of Jesus' childhood that have been brought together for the first time in one place and sequenced so that the reader will see a new picture of the early years of Jesus. If you only wish to read the stories of Jesus, skip directly to them in the text.

Finally, the bibliography is not only intended to be evidence of the existence of the records on Jesus' childhood, but to be a beginning foothold for the curious who wish to pursue Jesus' lost biography.

ORIGINAL SOURCES

The original sources for these stories include Matthew (the apostle), James (the older brother of Christ), and Thomas (the younger brother of Christ). It is not my intent to use them as scripture, or to prove or disprove anything beyond the existence of the stories themselves. Whatever conclusions should be drawn from these stories is left for the reader to find within himself. The material presented in this book will show you the water, but it is you who must decide whether or not to drink. Powerful hidden agendas have kept these accounts secret long enough. Surely the life of Jesus extended far beyond Christianity. The eyes of the whole ancient world were upon Jesus from many different countries, perspectives and religions, maybe even more so than they are today.

If the newspapers of the world were to print banner headlines that someone had mysteriously discovered additional words and stories of Jesus in the sands of the desert somewhere, or located them in some dusty archive in the basement of a church, there would be such clamor for access that no doors or locks could bar the public. Surprise!!! There have been several recent discoveries of enormous Christian libraries in the dust of the desert and incredibly many precious hidden records have been found in dusty archives of churches (3, 13, 17, 22, 24, 33, 35, 38, 39, 40, 42, 43, 44, 46, 48, 57, 61, 64, 65, 67). Jesus speaks to us in these documents like a voice from the dust. These writings are discoveries for the common man to whom Jesus was sent, and do not come directly to us from any powerful hidden agendas.

To put it into perspective, the world has rediscovered far more words of Jesus and stories about His life recorded outside the Bible, than there are contained in the Bible. Contrary to the resistant attitude of some, the Bible is not in jeopardy of being found a fraud. It is actually vindicated by these additional witnesses of Jesus. Even if the powerful are not excited about it, the common man will be glad for this window into the life of Christ, regardless of whether or not it bears a little sand from the desert, or dust from the basements of old churches. These discoveries are so rewarding that men may even forgive those who caused the documents to be hidden in the first place (33, 35, 42, 43, 60, 64). These documents were not written by the churches of the world, or by journalists, scientists or historians. They were written by the imperfect friends and family of Jesus himself--those who wanted us to know Him as they did.

APOCRYPHA—A MODERN SECRET

First of all, some of these lost or hidden records fall under the broad umbrella of Apocrypha (33, 35, 42, 43, 60, 64), which originally meant, "ONE TOO SACRED AND SECRET TO BE IN EVERYONE'S HANDS". The term Apocrypha is one of the most misunderstood concepts of modern lay Christianity. It has come to include a very large collection of works, much more than might be found as addendum in a Catholic Bible, and even more than the books that represent themselves to be The Apocrypha. If you go to the public library looking for Apocrypha, you will be astonished at the number of different combinations of documents that represent themselves as "The Apocrypha". The immediate question for the common man should be, "Why are there so many different combinations?" One can just imagine the many differences that existed in the scriptural libraries of the various churches after the death of Christ. To this day, trying to find a complete collection of "The Apocrypha" is not possible for the common man. The very best printed collections refer to other documents that the collectors themselves do not include in their books and will not even review.

After glancing into the abundant records listed in the bibliography, some readers will ask themselves the question, "If we have a lot more information about the birth and infancy of Jesus, why is the story in the Bible so incomplete?" Several people, members of Jesus' family and a couple of apostles, wrote the details of the childhood of Christ (48, 60, 61). After all, they lived with Jesus. Their records are not in the Bible. It is sadly evident that some of those in control of the final Canon of scripture did not share what they themselves possessed for reasons of their own (40, 48, 50). Hence, we are left with the job of finding those stories for ourselves almost two thousand years later.

The Apocrypha was originally held in the highest esteem by those much closer to the source than we are. However, over centuries of established Christian tradition, "Apocrypha" has come to mean something less than sacred, or even something less than truthful (19, 60, 61). The simple truth about ancient documents is that they are all less than perfect, even the Bible itself. After all, the recording of scripture has always been a human effort, even when it was inspired of God. Any discussion of perfection in the scriptures is like saying that the ocean is pure. Metaphorically speaking, it is. It, too, was created and preserved by God. However, a microscopic evaluation of either would show them to be filled with a mixture of complex life in its beauty and frailty.

We are not the only generation to have seen The Apocrypha, though it has alternately emerged and been hidden, depending upon the political and religious climate of the times (41, 58). As the libraries have grown older, there have been many historical figures, much closer to the source of the documents, who have attested to seeing not only the original copies of some of the documents written in the hand of the original authors, but the entire provenance. The Gospels themselves lack the kinds of provenance that existed for some of these Apocryphal works.

Lastly, the Apocryphal studies by the most learned men of our time read like contemporary treatises on the origin of the documents, rather than focusing on the content of the documents themselves. A document's origin should not be the only criteria for judging the truthfulness of the content. A good investigator will occasionally find very good evidence in very common locations. We don't ignore diamonds because they were originally found in the dirt. For example, The Gnostic Library at Nag Hammadi that was found in the sands on the bank of the Nile River has more sayings of Jesus than we possess in the Bible (48, 49, 57). Should we ignore them because they passed through the hands of

Christians who were not the direct ancestors of traditional Christian beliefs? In the case of The Apocrypha, those possessing these non-canonized documents during various times in history were subject to ridicule, censure and even martyrdom. No wonder these documents are coming to us from some very unusual places and directions.

The common public would rather hear the story than review the critique. We live in a time when we are weary of powerful entities hiding information and keeping secrets because they think we, the public, have no need to know. The public is tired of being ignored in the adjudication process to determine which documents are true and false. Most of us are able and willing to take the good and the bad in stride. We can make our own judgments about things and find meaning in the broad picture of events. The public is used to looking for fire when they see enough smoke in the air. While the version of the stories presented in this book may not have been preserved with complete accuracy by the original authors, and are most certainly not complete, they are sufficiently referenced to give the interested reader a very good place to begin.

Chapter 2

FORCES THAT BROUGHT THE BIBLE TOGETHER

The fragmented Apocrypha never gained favor in the canonization process for a variety of reasons. One of the major criteria for inclusion in the Canon was how often a document was read in the churches. The common people could not read for themselves, nor were there copies generally available for those who could read, so the scriptures were regularly read to them in the churches (41). Some of the writings were read often and were included in the Canon. Others slipped into oblivion and became Apocrypha and even more obscure documents. None of the ancient Christian churches possessed all of the documents. In order to be included in the Canon of scripture, a document not only had to be authentic, but also had to be popular. There were times when power, rather than reason, reigned supreme. Without a broad and unified base of support, some of the most precious and revealing documents were simply ignored (22, 41, 45, 57).

Over the course of three hundred years, groupings of separate documents gradually became associated with each other and gained separate loyal followings. For example, there was a group who exclusively supported the first four Gospels of the New Testament. The supporters of these documents were adamant that the New Testament should remain with only those four. This mimics the ancient Jewish Sadducees who were adamant that their scriptures only contain the five books of Moses.

If some early Christian powers had been given their way, the Bible's treatment of the life of Jesus would have been even more brief than it is today (7, 25, 41).

Another group supported the letters of Paul, which he sent to the churches which he visited. The letters of Paul were so widely accepted by the separate Christian churches that they were very hard to ignore in the final Canon, even though some of his letters were less popular and, therefore, were not included. Each of these groups wanted to include their favorite sacred writings and exclude everyone else's. To have your group's favorite scripture included in the Canon was a way of gaining power, rather than being careful to preserve all the information available, as one might think they should have done.

In the end, the ecumenical Councils of Nicea, in and around 325 A.D., put the final seal of approval on the Canon with a powerful and final vote. It is interesting to note that the Roman emperor Constantine had only declared Christianity the official state religion in 313 A.D. After the vote, it became politically unwise to discuss other, non-canonized documents. For example, Arius was commanded by the Bishop of Alexandria during the first council of Nicea to stop his discussions of additional documents or be declared a heretic.

There were no Popes elected until the sixth century. The manner of succession to authority in secular Christianity took a long time to be formalized. The political regional bishops, who were the ecclesiastic ruling council at the time, were the ones who voted on the Canon. Officially being declared a heretic by any Bishop of the Church was the end of life for these religious men. There was no second chance or defense offered, and no understanding given. In the end, the writings of Arius were largely destroyed.

The ancient theme of power and suspicion continues in the modern commentaries on Apocrypha, almost as if there are still powerful entities waiting to declare those who reveal these "hidden" documents as modern heretics. We can see this bizarre behavior when most of the formal investigations of additional words and stories of Jesus are still accompanied with an informal apology or denial of one sort or another (7). What are they afraid of? Are they afraid that the documents might have errors, or are they afraid that they might contain some truth? What if they have both errors and truth at the same time? It is very easy to condemn the weaknesses of The Apocrypha and ignore those very same types of weaknesses in the Bible. The reality is that many of those who deal with The Apocrypha today are still afraid of the potential condemnation of their own churches or of the scholars from around Christendom. Who are these scholars and churchmen that we should fear them? One of the reasons for writing this book is to eliminate this bias for the common reader. Maybe the common man is not as ignorant as the pious, or the learned, might think.

MIGRATION OF DOCUMENTS

Before the Canon was completed, individual books of scripture migrated, with the disbursement of the people, as far away as Europe, Africa, Asia, the Far East, and, of course, the varied Middle East (41). Mohammed, for example, had the stories of the infancy and ministry of Christ in his hands and included some of them when he wrote the Koran (Qur'an) in the sixth century (1). These stories of Jesus were so powerful that the Moslem Religion could not ignore Jesus, who was a distant relative within the family of Abraham. The Jews feel much the same as the Moslems about the powerful Jesus. Both the Moslem and Jewish religions believe Him to be a prophet, even though they don't accept the whole story. It is interesting to note that the Koran has references to the life of Jesus that both do, and do not, appear in the Bible. They had their own provenance for their infancy stories of Jesus (1, 7, 49).

The Moslems believe themselves to be unique among the peoples of the world in that they believe that the heavenly messengers exclusively visited them after the death of Christ. The reality is, however, that there are dozens of groups that also felt themselves unique because they experienced heavenly manifestations for themselves (19, 21, 44). Why wouldn't God be concerned with all the families of the earth? Most of these religious groups reject the claims of the other as if they had the exclusive relationship with God. The Moslems find Jesus wanting in terms of divine origin and resurrection, but they do not deny the virgin birth, or the miraculous power of Jesus. Half a story is better than none in this case. The Moslems believe their Christian brothers had strayed from the traditions of Abraham, the father of both Isaac and Ishmael, by the sixth century and that Christians should return to the family fold under the protection and guidance of Allah. The Christians believe that they were the "chosen family" of Abraham's two sons, and that Jesus, the prophet of the Moslems, belongs to them alone. The oneness of an ancient bickering family is most apparent to a completely neutral observer. These three great religions of the world do not accept each other, although they had the same original God, and have huge amounts of common ancestry and scripture.

Buddhism has also been influenced by Christianity, though it does not believe in a supreme being. At least we do not have an argument with the Buddhist over the name of God, or arguments over which brother received the real birthright. The Buddhists were influenced by the tradition of the Christian Gnostics, in that they knew of Jesus, the prophet King, and felt that spirituality originates from within the individual and not necessarily from the hierarchy of the church (56, 67). The trade routes between east and west carried with them religious teachings as well as products. These trade routes went through Egypt, India and Persia, all of which bore Gnostic Christian influences. These trade routes also became escape routes for Christians and Jews fleeing the Roman armies (50). Some who escaped from the Roman massacres traveled far away to the east and have been almost lost to history, along with their sacred libraries (7, 13-17, 19, 32, 41, 49).

One of the Magi who visited Jesus' birth came from Persia. There were miraculous heavenly manifestations foretelling Jesus' birth within the Persian temples before He was ever born. The star guided this Magian to the birthplace of Jesus only after his scriptures and heavenly manifestations foretold the specific events of the coming of the great King in Israel (19). He obviously possessed prophecy about the events that were to occur, though he didn't belong to either the Jewish, or the eventual Christian, religion.

One of the Magi came from India and another from Arabia. They, too, had scriptural reasons for their pilgrimage to Jesus' birth place, though they started and ended their religious lives outside traditional Christianity (19). Do we really expect that some of the most important men of the world would arbitrarily follow some bright new star without having a very real reason for doing so? Each of the Magi took home with him his own stories of Jesus to his own people. Bits and pieces of the stories of Jesus have crept into, or been an original part of, many of the great religions of the world (19).

There are amazing accounts of Jesus in ancient Europe (19, 36, 37, 54). For example, there is strong and varied evidence that the mother Mary herself, along with Mary Magdalene, Martha, Mary of Cleophas (Mary's sister-in-law), Lazarus (whom Jesus raised from the dead) and others, escaped the massacre of the Roman legions and the expulsion order of the Sanhedrin in 36 A.D., by fleeing to Britain after the death of Christ, with the help of her wealthy uncle, Joseph of Arimathea (19, 36). John the apostle, who was entrusted with Mary's welfare as Christ hung on the cross, was hotly pursued after the crucifixion and he had a dangerous mission to perform. John orchestrated the help of Joseph of Arimathea to protect Mary, although Joseph of Arimathea had already played an important family role in the lives of both Mary and Jesus after the death of Joseph (Mary's husband).

Joseph of Arimathea was a very significant personality in the background of Christianity and of history as a whole. Joseph of Arimathea provided his own personal tomb for the burial of Jesus and was one of those who transported the lifeless Jesus from the cross to his own resting place and who originally prepared the body (19, 60). Joseph of Arimathea was also a legislative member of the Sanhedrin, a provincial Roman Senator, one of the richest men in his time, and "Noblis Decurio" (19, 36). Decurio was a title given to a provider of metal products for the Roman empire (mostly tin and lead). Noblis Decurio was the Chief Provider. Cicero remarked that it was easier to be a Roman Senator than Noblis Decurio. Many of Joseph's tin and lead mines were located in Gaul of England. There is little wonder why Joseph of Arimathea chose England as the escape route for the protection of these prominent disciples (19, 36).

The apostle Philip spent a great deal of time with Mother Mary and the famous disciples when he was appointed to Gaul in England during his ministry, although he was martyred at Hierapolis. Paul's letters to the Galatians were often thought to be written to Gaul itself, rather than for just its political province of Galatia in the Near East. Paul and Luke also personally visited Gaul in England during their ministries. England was like a new home among friends for these men.

Joseph of Arimathea eventually became known as the "Apostle to Britain." England became known as the Sacred Isle, the Motherland, and "the most hallowed ground on earth", because of the prominent congregation following Christ's death. Mother Mary and her companions took with them personal accounts of Jesus, and they left stories throughout Europe (37, 42, 54, 59). Some of these stories sparked the crusades and became an integral part of the sacred liturgy of Medieval Europe.

The illustrious nature of the congregations in England gave the eventual Christians of England bragging rights to having the earliest Christian church. They were practicing Christianity long before the Romans began turning to Christianity in 196 A. D. The Church of England does not strictly consider itself a protestant religion. Its members had been faithful followers of Christ during Roman extermination orders and never needed a repentant change to be included in the Christian fold, as the Romans and Greeks later did. There is a cathedral in Britain, "Our Lady's Dowry," or St. Mary's Chapel, that claims to be built on the tomb of the Mother Mary, rather than at the Chapel of Dorminton near Jerusalem, where many of the non-Britain Christians claim it to be. The tomb is probably in England because of all the evidence, rather than at Dorminton, where the evidence has collapsed. There is an "Altar of Wattle" on the same site as the tomb of Mary in Britain that bears another impressive secret that will be left for those who are not faint of heart and who wish to pursue the records listed in the bibliography (19, 36).

When hundreds of thousands of people are running for their lives, as was frequently the case for the new Christians and the Jews of many eras, they could have ended up almost anywhere. These fleeing people would naturally take their religious histories with them. Few know that the Sadducean factions of the Sanhedrin that were directly responsible for the death of Jesus expelled all the remaining faithful followers of Jesus from the Holy Land in the "Exodus of the Faithful" in 36 A.D., about four years after the crucifixion. Where did they all go? Can there be any doubt why most of the scriptures we have today come from everywhere else but Judea, excepting of course the Dead Sea Scrolls that were buried by the radical Essenes who had been visited in the desert by Jesus and the apostles.

Heavenly prognostications not only prompted the Magi in the temples of Persia and in Mohammed's drawing room, but occurred around the world wherever the children of God were ready to listen. For example, Columbus recorded in his own diary that he was greeted on the islands of the Caribbean by Native American Indians who venerated him because they thought that he was the white-bearded God that promised their ancestors that he would return. The Aztecs in Mexico laid down their weapons for the conquering Conquistadors because they thought their Savior had returned (30).

Why didn't the Native American Indians fight back? They certainly would later raise a weapon or two when they were pushed and shoved around the Americas. There were millions of Indians killed throughout North and South America by comparatively small Spanish forces who fit into a few ocean vessels. The Indians could have stoned the Spanish to death with that many people, even if they had no weapons at all, which they most assuredly did. Conquistadors record that the Indians not only gave up their weapons voluntarily, but welcomed the murderous invaders into their midst with open arms. Eventually, it was easier for the native American Indian population to embrace

Christianity than any other conquered peoples of any era because of their own traditions. The ancient stories of the American Indians have many of the biblical stories in their lore.

The Rig-Vedas, the holy books of India, record that Jesus visited them in Nepal. This visit is also mentioned in the Vishnu Purana. It appears that Jesus visited India in His lifetime, while accompanying His wealthy merchant uncle, Joseph of Arimathea. Joseph sold metal to more peoples than just the Romans. That is a story that eludes Christians of modern eras and is a most impressive one.

NATURE OF ORIGINAL CHURCH

Some experts have estimated that there were more Christian sects in the first two centuries after Christ than there are today. The Romans did a fine job of dispersing the believers with their massacres and threats. When the Romans turned their hearts away from murder and hatred and embraced the impressive growing Christianity, the center of one of the largest amalgamations of churches gravitated to the North and West of Israel. This gathering of churches under one central authority is a story in and of itself. Romans and Greeks were famous for gathering people under one authority and not tolerating dissent. They adopted the idea that the church was the only entity that could, or should, be responsible for the spiritual welfare of the individual and for the preservation of scripture. When Rome gained control of a large part of the church, everyone either believed as they did, or they became a heretic and didn't have any right to a belief in Jesus. This group we will refer to as the Structuralists. They became the origins of Catholic, Greek Orthodox, Russian Orthodox, Coptic and eventually protestant religions.

These strongly centralized organizations preserved these religions following the death of Christ, though they were strongly influenced by Roman and Greek traditions. We know, for example, Christmas was being celebrated on December 25 to coincide with a traditional Roman holiday. The 25th of December

26

was not the real birthday of Jesus. The real birth of Jesus was in the spring of the year. Every religion of the time was influenced by local politics and traditions. If we were able to stand far enough away from our modern Christian religions, we would be astonished at how much ancient cultures and governments have influenced our current beliefs. We should be thankful to these churches for their preservation of the traditions of Christ, even if, because of human nature, they preserved some of their own country's traditions in the process.

One of the first examples of Christians turning on their own kind came with the Gnostic Christians, who believed that religion came from within the individual and disdained strong central control of any kind, especially Roman. The word Gnostic means "knowledge" or "one who knows". The people at the center of the Gnostic movement went south into Egypt and were largely massacred by the pursuing Roman armies, or vanished because of their lack of central organization. These Gnostic Christians were eventually branded as heretics by their northern brothers, though their origins and many of their scriptures were the same. The ancestors of the Structuralists murdered these Christians in their flight and later the Structuralists expelled them from their faith. The Gnostics had a real reason to not want to be a part of Roman beliefs. The Gnostics have long been the object of Christian ridicule because of some of their strange practices towards the end of their existence (50). The Structuralists still continue their assault on the Gnostic Christians. We shouldn't confuse the ending condition of a Christian religion with its origins any more than we should confuse the condition of Christianity today with its origin. You could easily imagine what happens to a church over hundreds of years.

One of the Gnostic libraries from the second century was found at Nag Hammadi on the banks of the Nile river in 1945 where it had been buried since the fourth century, upstream from the ancient Egyptian library at Alexandria on the Mediterranean coast. Alexandria experienced many different Christian influences over the centuries—Gnostic, Coptic and Structuralist. These Nag Hammadi documents are among the very oldest and most original accounts of Jesus of any known on earth—older than any Bible text. We see not only a strong influence of Gnosticism in the orient from these documents, but see a great deal of influence on the emerging Moslems who lived in the neighborhood five hundred years after Christ. If someone wanted to read just the words of Jesus, he would find the Nag Hammadi more voluminous by several times than the Bible. The Gnostic libraries had a far more concentrated focus on the life of Christ than the Bible of the Structuralists.

CANONIZATION OF SCRIPTURES

The Structuralists were responsible for the selection of the documents that make up the New Testament. In all fairness to the Structuralists, the decision of what to include in the Bible was complicated. The issues were much broader than the decisions of which books were true and which writings were false. The truthfulness, or authenticity, of the excluded documents is more a question of modern Christianity than it was for the compilers of the Canon. The Canon conferences were plagued by politics and piety. There was no effort on the part of the conferences of Nicea, nor from any subsequent era but our own, for that matter, to locate all the documents in the fragmented churches. Structuralists just naturally assumed that if a document existed they would possess it. They believed they possessed the only "pipeline" to God and, therefore, God would not let them ignore important scripture.

There was an arrogant omniscient feeling and a sense of urgency that allowed many precious documents to fall through the cracks. Remember that the difference of time between 313 A. D., when Constantine declared Christianity a state religion, and 325 A.D., the date of the beginnings of the Nicea Councils, was only twelve years. The Bible was not only a long time in coming, but in the end was a kind of "rush job" as well.

The men in attendance at the Nicean conferences ignored the fact that the Bible referred to additional documents within its internal structure. They also held many documents secret for themselves, feeling that the public couldn't handle it all. Lastly, there were large bodies of documents that simply lost out in the final vote. It is amazing how some Christians of today hang their "shingle" exclusively and defensively on the vote of such a political and pious group. If God was inspiring these men to exclude some of the records of the life of Christ, the logic eludes me. The scriptures were inspired, but the treatment of them certainly was not!

Many of the records, though written by credible people like the apostles, where written as stories rather than in other, more formal, formats. Stories were not intended to be formal doctrinal statements and often included metaphors and allegory that could not be taken literally. Some of the stories written by the apostles were taken from original apostolic notes, as was the case of the source concept called the "Q". The "Q" was a compilation of notes and oral tradition the apostles used to write their gospels (41). The stories were developed over a few decades following Christ, and at least two of them, Matthew and Luke, became original Gospels of the Bible itself.

The bishops felt that they were the only ones that could understand and appreciate the original notes and stories. For example, Matthew wrote not only the gospel contained in the Bible, but stories of Jesus' childhood contained in this book. The Gospel he wrote was canonized, but the stories he wrote were not to be read by the general public and were held for private reading of the "Lord's anointed." The Book of James, or the Protevangelium, was written by the brother of Jesus, and contains a most illuminating account of the infancy of Christ and His own family. Many of the writings of James were excluded from the Canon. Two books on the infancy of Christ were written by Thomas, the younger brother of Jesus, an individual who still had doubts about Jesus' resurrection until he had touched the risen Savior's hands and feet. Contained in the Gnostic libraries is a very valuable Gospel of Thomas that was excluded from the Bible, though it is very doctrinal in content. There have been many scholars who have thought that this Gospel belongs in the Bible. The Gospel of Thomas resembles the illusive "Q" document and predates the Four Gospels themselves.

Most of those who wrote about Jesus had no idea that their words would be canonized or rejected by the religious future. The writers simply recorded the events of Jesus' life in their own words before they could be forgotten. We owe a great debt of gratitude to these storytellers, instead of treating them like dark family secrets. Some of the stories would not bear up under the microscope of professional journalism of today, but neither would the Bible for that matter. This does not mean that the stories are not true, or about real people and events, or that the writers were liars. The "one lie all lie" attitude is as ridiculous for mortal men as the "one truth all truth" philosophies. Neither of these positions are truthful in this imperfect world. Jesus can still be the Savior of the world even if some of his friends took a little editorial license in their retellings, and even if a bunch of books are missing from the Bible.

Selection and rejection of scripture from a larger body of work was not unique to the New Testament. There was a selection process for the Old Testament from a larger body of documents, also. In the early part of the first century B.C. a council of seven priests, representing each of the twelve tribes of Israel, was chosen to sift through the individual documents and to arrive at a compendium that could be universally accepted. The books of the Old Testament languished for millennium as single documents and never were intended to be bound in leather in one book by the original authors. We can only guess what those priests saw when they had the records of thousands of years in front of them. We are told that there may have been close to a million scrolls destroyed in the great fire of Alexandria. This was a mere seven decades before Jesus. Many of the Old Testament documents were housed where the council of priests made their selections just a couple of decades before the fire.

The fact that this body of priests traveled all the way from Israel to Egyptian Alexandria to make their selections reveals a lot about the nature of diverse libraries of scripture. Egypt played a very significant role for the Old Testament but was ignored in the eventual New Testament, though Jesus lived and performed miracles of importance there. Why did the Roman-based Christian bodies ignore Egyptian records of Jesus? Did the conflicts of Roman/Egyptian politics in the Cleopatra era of 46 B.C. have anything to do with that story? There are those who think so. The burning of the library in Alexandria was a loss of incalculable importance.

NATURE OF THE TEXT

Jesus himself often spoke in parables which were not necessarily about actual people or events (7, 41, 49). He didn't teach in this way to confuse us, or so that someone would have to translate for us. He spoke that way so that we would learn how to listen for ourselves. Some had "ears to hear", in the words of Jesus, and some didn't. This story method of teaching was important to Jesus Himself. His story-like parables require us to search for spiritual meaning, as if the process was as important as the discovery itself. The story format of this book parallels the original teaching style of Jesus.

The closer one gets to the Savior himself, as a source, the more unusual and miraculous the stories become. Some of us might think that the opposite would naturally be true. The distant Canon councils might have tended to embellish more than the eye witnesses. In this unique case, however, His closest friends spoke more robustly about His unique life. They often didn't have words or phrases sufficient to describe what they had seen with their eyes. The stories told by His friends are far more miraculous and unique in content than the accepted tradition of some of the more "tame" doctrinal documents the Canonizers favored, with the exception of the Book of Revelation. The Book of Revelation is the one maverick document that appears out of place in the Bible and was almost excluded from the Canon for reasons mentioned in a moment.

The authorship is no more suspect for the majority of the non-biblical documents than for the Bible. Some of the most dramatic events in the life of Jesus and His friends and family were just too much for succeeding generations to swallow for a variety

31

of reasons, not the least of which was that the stories offended existing cultures, traditions and faiths. It is interesting to note that the Canonizers rejected the book about the divine origins of the Mother Mary and left nothing in the canonized Bible to support their own beliefs of a deified Mary. A really good story sometimes comes across as if it is too much to handle, even when it does tend to support your traditions.

Chapter 3

INFLUENCES ON THE RECORDED LIFE OF JESUS

Hollywood has soft played the events of Christ's life, like it was some kind of a natural event with occasional divine overtones; just enough of the miraculous was left to make the life of Jesus worth watching. We, the public, are at fault for the behavior of Hollywood, because we are the ones who have to have a tangible, rational explanation for everything or we won't even watch the show. Truth is often far stranger than fiction.

Those who knew Jesus on a day-to-day basis were overwhelmed by the uniqueness of His daily life. He must have often appeared alien to them. Being the Son of God made His life appear, euphemistically speaking, sensational at the very least. Some of the people who heard Him speak and saw His miracles became His disciples when the mountain of tangible evidence required them to be so. Wherever He went, there were a variety of followers that valued being with Him more than their own homes, families and livelihoods. Some of these disciples were friends and family of the Sadducees who were the leaders of the Sanhedrin. The Sadducees were ultimately the ones who condemned Jesus to the cross. Some were so overwhelmed by His actions that they had to reject their eyes and ears or rewrite the definitions and methodologies of their whole life and culture. Some of these very confused people fought against Jesus to preserve the consistency of their homes, beliefs and traditions. We often fall into that latter category.

It often is a source of amazement that the modern disciples of Jesus are as defensive as children, not unlike their Jewish counterparts who crucified Christ rather than letting their eyes and ears access their hearts. Jesus would have invited all His sheep to follow Him, especially the lost ones. It is very likely that Jesus stands, unseen, in the center of us all and beckons to His people from His lofty place to extend an open hand and listening ear to one another.

The apologists over the years have attempted to smooth over the stranger sounding tales in an attempt to make them more palatable for the readers as a whole. There are events in the life of Jesus that may not make sense in our culture, or even in our own personal value systems. If Jesus was the Son of God, He represented a different system altogether than any we have had on the earth—one that valued money, authority, and even life differently than we do. The power of the Son of God on earth caused more than a few strange things to happen, besides the healing of a few sick people. The closest people to Christ told the stories like they saw it, and their writings have been hidden away like skeletons in the closet (19, 25, 36, 55, 61).

PROVENANCE OF SCRIPTURE

None of the Christian churches of today, even the oldest of them, have the entire provenance of their scriptures that can be traced to the actual paper and pen of the authors. There has been an intense search on the part of scholars to find a copy of the original Gospels. Part of the excitement of the discovery of the Dead Sea Scrolls and the Nag Hammadi Library has been a hope that there would be confirmation of the original gospel texts. Why are we all so excited to find confirmation of the original Gospel texts and condemn other documents because we only have copies?

The earliest Bibles we have in our possession are written in Greek, one of the languages common to the Structuralists, instead of the language of Jesus. Greece is located between Israel and Rome and the first place for the escaping Christians to visit on their

34

way west. The process of translation would logically proceed with the same geography. Greek was also used as the mediating language between different countries during this time of great ecumenical awakening.

The Rosette Stone found in Alexandria by Napoleon was the key to unlocking Egyptian Hieroglyphics. The ancient Greek writings on that stone, alongside the Egyptian hieroglyphics, was the key to unlocking the written language of the Pharaohs. Greek has also strangely become the key to unlocking the secrets to the New Testament.

The murderous Roman armies took care to destroy any libraries that might have existed in Israel in the mother tongues by 70 A.D. Roman armies were responsible for the destruction of recorded history wherever they went. If we are going to be touchy about provenance, then the issue of the original language is a major problem for the Bible itself. Where is the original Bible text in Hebrew or Aramaic, which were the languages of the Jews and of the merchant cities, like Galilee, to the north? It doesn't do to critique the provenance of the peripheral documents and ignore the similar provenance of the Bible. Everyone gets dirty in that mud fight. There shouldn't be a different standard to begin with. The message of the stories of Jesus can be heard by those with "ears to hear" from the smallest and most obscure accounts. Jesus often said so himself.

PREVENTION OF DISCOVERIES OF JESUS' WORDS

In an effort to prevent the public from searching for more scripture, some well-intentioned, and very protective, Church leaders of the third century sequenced the Book of Revelation at the end of the New Testament, as if God had intended it to be located there all along. They used the last phrase of warning with regard to additions and deletions, as if it applied collectively to all the very separate documents that were Canonized in the Bible. It is hard to imagine that the sequencing of the books of the New Testament was that divinely inspired. Surely John didn't leave a note to the Canon council to place his book at the end. If that were true, then the council should not have deleted any of the rest of the documents on the table. The whole story of Christmas and many additional stories and sayings of Jesus were on that table, too.

Serious scholars of the Bible discuss the fact that the Book of Revelation almost didn't make it into the final Canon because "it spoke of Millennium and was mysteriously vague." The vote was close on that one. Millennium was a concept they didn't understand. The concept of the Millennium required an understanding of apostasy. These men were just beginning to organize the infant church. They didn't want to discuss Jesus' prophecies about an apostasy that would require that which was hidden to be made known at some future time.

The Book of Revelation was an "odd duck" in the extreme when it came to the New Testament. The one reason it made it into the final text was because it was read so often to the public. There were many other Apocalyptic documents written by apostles that were not included in the Canon. The language of the Book of Revelation made a real impact on listening crowds. Its Apocalyptic message has been used as a religious weapon of fear for many groups who fell short of understanding the more important messages of Christ, like love, acceptance of all people, and the development of personal character.

What would the protective churches of the world have used as a weapon of control if the Book of Revelation had been left out of the Canon? Would they have found the other places in the middle of the same Bible that talk about deletions and additions and placed one of them at the end instead? What would have happened if one of the other Apocalyptic documents, written by one of the other apostles, had been chosen for the end of the Bible? There are several of these still in existence today. There is an Apocalypse of Peter, one of Paul, a couple by James, and even one reported by Adam himself.

Chapter 4

CHRISTIAN OBJECTIONS TO
ADDITIONAL DOCUMENTS

Language like, "Didn't God preserve His words for us in a complete and pure form?", is common for some of modern Christianity, when they refer to their exclusive belief in the Bible, while rejecting anything and everything else. It doesn't make sense to say, "We need no more Bible" when it is clear that "more" has always existed. Any discussion of "need" or "purity" denies the potential value and ignores the inherent problems with all the existing texts. A discussion of "need" or "purity" will neither make the rest go away, nor make the Bible any more important. The truth is that the Bible is clearly just part of what existed at, or near, the time of Christ.

We have allowed ourselves to be convinced by those with powerful agendas that the matter of the scriptures are above our heads and that outright rejection of anything not included in the Bible text is the safest course of belief. It is most apparent for anyone with an objective mind that God didn't abbreviate the story of His only begotten Son in the Bible. On the contrary, it is more reasonable to conclude that God would rather we have more so that we may be sufficiently informed.

The Bible itself mentions other books of scripture that are not included in the Canon. For Example: The Book of the Wars of the Lord (Num. 21: 14); The Book of Jasher (Josh. 10: 13; 2 Sam. 1: 18); The Book of the Acts of Solomon (1 Kgs. 11: 41);

The Book of Gad the Seer (1 Chr. 29: 29); The Book of Nathan the Prophet (1 Chr. 29: 29); The Prophecy of Ahijah (2 Chr. 9: 29); The Visions of Iddo the Seer (2 Chr. 9: 29); The Book of Shemaiah (2 Chr. 12: 15); The Book of Jehu (2 Chr. 20: 34); The Sayings of the Seers (2 Chr. 33: 19); an epistle of Paul to the Corinthians written earlier than our present 1 Corinthians (1 Cor. 5: 9); an earlier epistle to the Ephesians (Eph. 3: 3); an epistle to the Church at Laodicea (Col. 4: 16); The Prophecies of Enoch (Jude 1: 14); The Book of the Covenant (Ex. 24: 7); Samuel's The Manner of the Kingdom (1 Sam. 10: 25); The rest of the Acts of Uzziah by Isaiah (2 Chr. 26: 22). In addition, there are references to prophecy that do not appear in the Bible. For example, Matthew referred to the prophecy that Jesus would be a Nazarene (Matt 2: 23). This prophecy, told in the words of the original prophet, does not appear in the Bible. Where are all these books? Why didn't someone look for these documents before finalizing the Canon and establishing the provenance processes of the New Testament? Those of the early centuries would have had an easier time finding additional documents than we have some two thousand years later. If the original writers of the Bible felt these additional works were also scripture, who are we to ignore the fact that there were more books in existence?

Jesus had a very different style. He liked including the socially objectionable sayings of women and the obscure texts and beliefs of others in His teachings. He liked spending His personal time with foreigners, the lowly children, publicans and sinners and the sweet-spirited women. It wasn't Jesus' style to isolate Himself from others as we see some do today. Nor was it His style to ignore the broader-based teachings of many peoples because they weren't perfect. The only rejection recorded from the life of Christ was the rejection of those with hatred, pride or greed. These are the sins most frequently addressed in our own Bible, and yet they are the very sins which strangle the message of Christ in our modern religious practices. These are the qualities that hide inside men until we take a good look in a mirror and have "eyes to see". It might be more productive to ask the question, "Who owns Christ?" The real answer might soften many hearts.

One of the other arguments that is used for rejecting other non-biblical documents has been that "We need no more Bible because we can get the message of God from the smallest of fragments." If the message of Jesus is available in the smallest of fragments in the Bible, one shouldn't have problems with more small fragments. The fact that the story of Jesus' birth to young adulthood in the Bible is so very brief should cause some suspicion and curiosity. What could we learn from the rest of the story?

There is an enormous question that we all should ask ourselves. Where are the unencumbered investigative journalists for the life of the Savior? Are the royalty of England or the private lives of movie stars and politicians the only areas of curiosity? Do the churches of the world have so much influence over everyone's thinking that it keeps us from wanting to know more about Jesus? Does one have to be a well coached or learned scholar to be curious about Jesus? Is it possible that there has been a massive cover up of documents and that the cover-up still persists today? The answer should become clear once a person has spent some time in the bibliography.

NOT A SINGLE MASTER COPY

Somehow many people of today have the mistaken opinion that the scriptures were sequestered and preserved in one location, like there was one master book from which all the subsequent copies were duplicated. This is a great error in perception. There were many different libraries at any given point in time, and later a variety of Bibles for that matter. After all, the word "Bible" means many books. Each of the churches that were established by the apostles had their own written records (41, 51, 60). The Bible was pieced together from the collections inside these churches. Local churches loved to exchange copies of sacred documents and letters among themselves. Occasionally, they liked to keep some to themselves alone. There were no photocopy machines or printing presses in those days. Each of the documents they possessed from the hands of the apostles were unique, and so were their libraries.

DESTRUCTION OF DOCUMENTS

There were many different destructions of precious documents that chronicled our Christian past, besides the fire in Alexandria Egypt. The massacre by the Romans in 70 A.D. murdered countless new Christians and Jews alike and destroyed or scattered their libraries. This was one "Holocaust" that was shared by Jews and Christians alike.

Around 200 A. D., the Roman Christians burned most of the religious texts written by and about women in public fires, because of their cultural bias against women extended into their religious beliefs. These were new Christians who still clung to some of their old traditions and were offended by some of the brand new concepts that required them to change some very traditional structures of their own homes. Jesus Himself arbitrated arguments between Mary Magdalene and Peter over the influence of women in the life of Jesus. We have some of those accounts in the Magdalene documents. Jesus' response to Peter's attitudes toward women reads like a brief contemporary treatise on the spiritual importance of women. There is abundant evidence that Jesus had problems with some of the attitudes of His own apostles from time to time, especially as it pertained to women.

After Jesus was resurrected, He spent forty days with His apostles and His closest disciples before His final ascension to heaven, teaching them about things they should have known to begin with. This forty-day ministry became the source of motivation for His disciples, who had denied Jesus to their enemies, or had returned to their old jobs when Jesus was arrested and crucified (19, 36). The women in Jesus' life were different. They were the natural believers and demonstrated more faith than the apostles themselves. It was the women in the life of Jesus whom He chose to visit first after He had been resurrected.

Some scholars have claimed that Jesus was a "womanizer" because of His association with hundreds of women disciples. Of course this was not true. Jesus and His Heavenly Father authored the moral codes of the Ten Commandments. The reality of Jesus' life was that He was often criticized for traveling in the company of dozens of women disciples, rather than exclusively with male apostles and disciples, as was expected of His Jewish upbringing and tradition. Orthodox Jews still separate their women into the balcony of their synagogues. Part of the reason Jesus was called a "womanizer" was that He is cited as kissing Mary Magdalene while in the public streets. It wasn't acceptable to kiss anyone of the opposite sex in public—even your wife. This kissing incident caused more problems for Jesus than His miracles, and almost as much as His claim to be the Son of God.

There was a very special relationship between Mary Magdalene and Jesus which is still a respectable, but not so well kept, secret of today (34, 57, 60). There is some suspicion that the crucifixion of Jesus had more to do with His friendly association with the wives of the Sanhedrin who would come to hear Him speak and work His miracles, than with the Sanhedrin's objections to Jesus healing the sick. You can meddle with a lot of things in a man's life, but you meddle with the attitude of his wife, or his money, and you will get an irrational hatred of the kind we saw in Jerusalem at the time of the crucifixion. Give Jesus a little credit for being at least a partially mortal man. Just because He kissed a girl in the streets of Jerusalem shouldn't make Him a lecher. The women of Judea followed Jesus because of His powerful and meek acceptance of their status as human beings and very real members of the fraternity of the "children of God". Historically, women have always been more susceptible to spiritual matters than men of any era. Most of His disciples were, and should have been, women, because of their spiritual susceptibility.

The Gnostic writings that were missed by the Structuralist's purging fires of 200 A. D. include many positive female images that are now lost to modern Christianity. They even speak of the tremendous female presence in the heavens themselves (57). Women were often treated as second-class citizens in the desert world of Israel, as well as in the world of the Romans. They, unfortunately, are still considered second-class citizens in much of our own world. Jesus risked His very life and reputation by teaching us with His words and example about the parallel importance of women.

41

When Muhommad Ali al Samman, the little Arab child, found the Christian Nag Hammadi library inside earthen jars in caves near the banks of the Nile River in 1945, he used some of them for fire wood. When someone found out how precious these documents would be to Christians and collectors, they were sold off "piece meal" to the four winds, and scholars had a very difficult political problem with their retrieval. These documents are saturated with Jesus' own words, unlike the narrow focus of our own Bible (57).

The huge Dead Sea Scroll libraries that have yet to be completely translated were left by the Essenes and have fallen into a deplorable state of disrepair over the millennium of laying in the dirt. There are many modern academic groups piecing that largely Old Testament puzzle together.

There must have been countless stories of destruction and loss of documents that are still secrets of history today. For example, the original documents that contained Matthew's account of Jesus and His family, included in this book, were preserved and seen in the handwriting of the original writers by bishops hundreds of years after the Romans had finished their destructions and long after the Canonizers were dead and forgotten. The original documents are likely still in the basement of a church somewhere.

The likely reason we do not have the original texts of many books is because they got old and fell apart. It should be no surprise that, given the length of time that has passed, we are left with only copies of copies. In addition, there are a number of highly secret and well guarded vaults of documents in several locations around the world that probably possess the crumbling remains of many original Christian writings.

Chapter 5

JESUS WAS FAMOUS IN EGYPT

Jesus was a "Hit" in Egypt during His life, unlike the suspicion He felt from His own home town, causing Jesus to avoid publicity among His neighbors. The family of Jesus caused such a sensation in Egypt that it is embarrassing that some of the events from that era in His life are not in the Bible. The infant Jesus healed the leprous son of at least one of the prominent rulers of Egypt. He and His family lived in the company of the Pharaoh's family in Egypt, who were far more accepting of the powerful Jesus than His own neighbors in Judea.

The angel told Joseph to take his family to Egypt to escape the murderous rage of Herod. Why couldn't Jesus have just hidden out among His own people or in the wilderness somewhere, like the infant John the Baptist did? John the Baptist was the object of Herod's quest anyway. Herod thought that the great King of the Jews would be the son of a high priest in the temple. For this reason he killed Zacharias in the temple when he wouldn't reveal where his son was. Is it possible that the angel knew of the great work Jesus would do among the Egyptians? Again, where is that complete story in the Bible? Some of that story clearly exists to this day, written by His apostles.

The angels in heaven told many of those who had been healed or had seen Jesus' miracles in His home town to keep their experiences hidden as a protective device for Jesus, though He didn't need such protection in Egypt or other places where He visited and worked His miracles. Some have thought that He kept some of His miracles a secret out of modesty, or because they were sacred, private experiences. We must remember, however, that His mission was to be the Savior of the world and not necessarily to be the private healer of the sick. The secrecy of some of His works were never intended to be permanently secret. The accounts summarized in this book tell of some of these intentionally staggered disclosures. Jesus himself said that there were hidden things that would eventually be made known. The secrecy was designed for a much more political reason.

BIRTH AND LIFE ARE SMALL PART

If you glance at the narrative in the New Testament regarding the birth of Jesus and His childhood, you will find that it occupies one page. How can this be when Jesus is supposedly the focus of the Bible with its hundreds of pages?!? Jesus didn't suddenly begin His life at the age of thirty. His life was a barrage of incredible tales from birth. From birth to the age of twelve, the story of Jesus in the New Testament reads like a brief aside, rather than a scriptural account that is intended to be the focus for all of our lives. Someone really "goofed" when they ignored the "growing up" years of Jesus' life in the Canon. There are dozens of scholars who criticize the Bible, though they are Christians themselves, because it conspicuously lacks the narrative of Jesus' whole life.

The Canon was never intended to be the exclusive doctrine of the apostles or only a description of their acts. Why do we have more information in the Bible about the life of Moses than Jesus himself? Fortunately, the missing story of the life of Jesus is not yet a totally lost secret, though it does take a mind that is accepting of documents beyond the Bible to find it.

For the first time in the public forum, these stories tell about His abilities from the time He was born. Jesus was revered as the foremost scholar of all time by some of the most educated men in His own country (19, 36, 60). Contrary to common belief,

Jesus even wrote letters in His own hand. Some of these writings were copied and are just now being rediscovered. Before the age of the Apocalyptic era prophesied in the Book of Revelation, Jesus must emerge from His lost status and be revealed as the integral part of the lives of people around the world. However, this cannot happen with closed minds, or with possessive attitudes toward the records. Some will have "ears to hear" and some will not. Some of those who profess to be His modern disciples will need to broaden their horizons. Will they wait until they can touch His hands and feet before they will get the point?

Jesus didn't always work as a carpenter with His earthly father during His life. His family had divinely inspired wealth from not only their own personal fortunes as descendants of the Hebrew Royal Family, but from the gifts of gold from the Magi and gold from the rulers of Egypt, where the infant Jesus healed their sick children (19, 60). Being a carpenter was more than just building fences or wooden utensils. Joseph built homes for the wealthy and other projects for kings, much like building contractors today (19, 36, 60).

There is serious doubt that Jesus continued as a carpenter after the death of His earthly father, Joseph. When Joseph had died Jesus spent a lot of time with His extremely wealthy uncle, Joseph of Arimathea. There appears to be some confusion over which "Joseph" Jesus was with during different times of His life. Jesus traveled on a ship or two during His life with His uncle, who owned fleets of vessels. The traveling Jesus is still being kept a secret by those in control of His biography, though Jesus is mysteriously quoted in the flesh in records far distant from Judea. There is one account, for the record, where Jesus is taxed as a foreigner because He had spent so much time out of the country with, and for, His uncle (19, 36). That could be one of the reasons His story as a young man is so absent in the Bible. He simply was not in the country a lot of the time.

INITIAL SHOCK TO READER

There may be some initial shock to the reader when he finds these stories add subtle facts and ideas that change the traditional image of the Holy Family. For example, Joseph was reported from many sources to have been much older than the fifteen-year-old Mary, and a widower with four children (19). James and Simon are well known to have been brothers of Jesus, but few understand that they were His older brothers. The Roman Christians of the second century would not want you to know of Jesus' older sisters, Lydia and Lysia, who played a major role in His life and ministry and had already married and left the house when Jesus was born. Mary, the mother of Jesus, was often referred to as Mary of James because of her special parental relationship with Joseph's youngest son from his first wife, who was still a child when Joseph and Mary were married.

The selection of Joseph to be Mary's husband is a most miraculous story and is contained in this book. Mary later stood without her husband by her side at the feet of the crucified Jesus, because her husband Joseph had died (19, 60). His death chronicles an interaction between Jesus, His family, the angels, and His apostles, that has long been a hidden secret and a revealing example of Jesus' divine position. That story is also contained in this book.

The age discrepancy between Mary and Joseph should not diminish the love story between the earthly parents of Jesus. There have been generations of scholars who have rejected documents on the life of Joseph for that very reason alone. Does it make Jesus any less divine because His earthly father was married before? Are the widowers and widows of our society less pure than those who have never been married? There were some cultures at the time of Jesus, and much later, who felt that way. Should we reject Joseph because he was much older than Mary? It wasn't Joseph's idea to court Mary to begin with. The facts could not be changed, but they could be ignored. The mother of Jesus was a virgin, but the earthly father of Jesus had an existing family (19, 60). Many of the realities surrounding the life of Christ contain this kind of contrasting examples for us all.

Some of the details will expand upon the stories presented in the Bible. For example, the biblical birth of Jesus leads us to believe that Jesus was born in a stable next to an inn. The infancy stories of Jesus reported in this book have Him born in a cave just outside Bethlehem near the ancient tomb of Rachel, because Mary couldn't wait. Today if you visit the birthplace of Jesus in Bethlehem many people are surprised that they are led to the remnants of a cave and not some pasture or sequestered part of an ancient city building. Joseph and Mary left the cave after the birth of Christ and went to the inn inside the city of Bethlehem, where they had to stay in the stable because there were no vacancies due to the many travelers arriving there to pay their taxes. Hotel space in a small town was limited at best. From the biblical birth story, Jesus may appear to have humble beginnings, but that was circumstantial evidence and not the truth. Joseph could easily have afforded the price of a room at any inn he chose. Joseph and Mary stayed at inns for most of the time they were exiled in Egypt. Try living in a hotel today for a couple of years. If they had really been poor, they would have stayed in the countryside, like others of modest means did. It was to the stable next to the inn in Bethlehem that the shepherds came and to Bethlehem that the Magi later brought their gifts.

Whether Jesus was born in a cave or a stable built of wood and straw isn't as important as the tremendous expansion of the narrative of the birth of Jesus. For the first time the stories in this book chronicle more of the details that happened surrounding the early life of Jesus. Hang on to your seat, because this additional story is told from a very different perspective. It happened during the day time.

The birth story, for example, includes a midwife. This midwife, Solome, followed Jesus throughout His life and became an important member of Jesus' disciples. She even fled with the Baby Jesus and His family into Egypt to escape the murderous jealousy of King Herod and eventually fled with the Mother Mary into Britain (19, 36, 49, 60).

Sometimes the documents reveal several versions of the same story. For example, there is the story of the visit of Mother Mary and the Child Jesus to the dye shop. Several different versions exist. In one version Jesus puts the shopkeeper's "cloths" into a furnace. In another, Jesus puts the "cloths" into a vessel of black dye. In both cases, however, the story reads essentially the same and has the same outcome. Who knows, maybe these are separate incidents.

Chapter 6

AUTHOR'S PURPOSE

There are volumes of stories and words of Christ outside the Bible. However, the author has chosen just the stories of the life of the infant Jesus and His family that have never been widely read before. The more doctrinal adult life of Jesus is left for another time. It is not my intent to write scripture—only to tell the untold stories. Taste a bit, hear a bit, and reject or accept as you please. It is time that the general public becomes the "one who knows" like the philosophy of the Christian Gnostics of old. Let the public decide this one for themselves for the first time, without a powerful agenda filtering what we read.

I have returned the accounts of the childhood of Jesus to story form, as they were intended to be by the original authors. Nothing was added to the stories for any reason, though I have left many things in the original texts for the future discovery of the adventurous. These stories have been carefully brought together and sequenced. There is not only an additional visualization, but an economy in reading the entire story together on the same page.

There is ample bibliography to allow the more adventurous to go to the original sources for themselves. Many of the original books can be found in the larger public libraries, if you know where to look for them. The bibliography is just the front door to an enormous library of information.

In preparing this book, where there are two or more accounts of the same story, I merged elements of them all to fit the missing pieces together where they belong.

The unspoken agenda in these stories is for those who have "ears to hear." That agenda will emerge very differently for everyone. Do not let the adventure of something new frighten you. The real Jesus and His family are more exciting than the myth. If the stories make Jesus a much larger part of the real world and trigger a little more hope in your heart, the original authors will have accomplished their ancient purpose and so will I.

As the general public researches the original texts from whence this material was taken, they will have as many different opinions about the subject as there are readers. That will be a very natural outcome. Spirituality is a journey one must travel alone.

The churches of the world are to be congratulated on their dissemination of moral principles and the preservation of the teachings of Christ for all peoples. Without their efforts the message of Christ may have died. The life of Jesus has had enormous influence on our lives whether we believe in Him or not. The journey for spirituality doesn't stop, however, at the doors of the church. It must continue alone into the individual efforts and hearts of men.

ACADEMIA—A CASE AGAINST A MODERN INQUISITION

The most prominent critique for this little book is expected to come from the academic world. There was a hidden agenda in the preparation of this book. My intent is to return the story of Jesus to its proper perspective and to force investigators to analyze documents as they relate to each other, rather than keeping them isolated and defenseless against the onslaught of the modern "anointed" who view provenance as the only tool for authentication.

The general public must understand that there was a major "changing of the guard" during the 1960's. The search for Jesus was taken from the hands of the religious movements and from the sincere believers of the world and it landed inside the ivy halls of academia. The academics of the world seized control with hidden

50

agendas of their own, using as their excuse that they were the only ones that could objectively examine the discoveries. This same ancient rhetoric was used at least once before to keep the stories out of the hands of the general public.

The believing religious movements allowed this change of control because they didn't know what to do with documents that exceeded their traditions and which threatened the doctrinal foundations of their individual or specific beliefs. The ancient Structuralists, who gave us the Bible, used the very same language to seize control of the scriptures a couple of centuries following the death of Christ. They felt that the general public at that time was not competent to preserve or interpret the scriptures for themselves. The truth is that the academic scholars of the world are as biased as anyone on earth. They have their own faithless hidden agendas which have all but taken the miracle out of the most miraculous event in history.

Much of the recognition the academic receives comes from his role as skeptic. Skepticism is a process that fits well into the laboratory, much better than advocacy. Skepticism is the "lazy man's" approach to research, because most of the work has already been done in the discovery and advocacy process. Pardon the ugly analogy, but vultures love to leave the work of killing to nature and prey on carrion because it lies still and doesn't move. It is a much greater, and more productive, task to advocate and promote. Advocacy brings things to life. Skepticism is an attempt to devour. The process of advocating makes the advocate a big target in an academic world, while the process of criticism and skepticism is not so lonely. As a result of his environment, the academic is not traditionally as skilled or equipped to deal with the macrocosmic investigations of discovery, though he would deny this, in his arrogance, to anyone.

In all fairness to those in the academic world, they are amazingly skilled inside their own laboratories.

The so called "softer sciences", like phenomenology, are often scorned by segments of the academic world as contaminated processes. In essence, if something doesn't fall completely within the confines of one discipline, it has a tendency to be considered

51

"dirty". The Canon councils had a very similar attitude, in that the discussion of scriptures by the "unwashed" was considered corruption. Both academics and the Structuralists have missed the point and have polluted the scriptures with their own diseases.

Let us take an example. The word "myth" has crept into the books and research about Jesus written by the academics. The basis for the introduction of the word "myth" stems from the microcosmic analysis of Christianity as originating from, and belonging exclusively to, the Holy Land at the time of Christ. In simple language, if the story came from one small source, it is a "myth". Therefore, the story of Jesus is looked at as a regional legend which simply got out of hand. When looked upon with a microcosmic vision, the life of Jesus becomes literature, or myth, or a tale with mere social impact. However, the academics ignore the fundamental and obvious fact that there is a corroboration of Jesus in widespread ancient documents. The story of Jesus pervades a wide body of literature, culture, politics and even countries. Jesus was anything but a single individual who lived in the little country of Judea. The prophecies about Jesus extend through millennium and the whole geography of the earth.

A good phenomenologist sees Jesus as the one person with more impact on humanity than any single man who ever existed. The phenomenologists are like an American Indian chief who sits on the mountain and looks for God in the four winds, the trees, the ground and the sky. These phenomenologists find that Jesus emerges as a story that did not solely originate in Jerusalem, but rather appeared in the temples of Persia, in the jungles of Africa, on the isles of the sea, in the Americas from top to bottom, in the far east and indeed around the world, with no logical human progression. A myth does not act like that at all—to the contrary.

A myth doesn't suddenly appear in the modern literature on Near Death Experience. A myth doesn't suddenly receive confirmation in double blind studies in the San Francisco hospitals that studied the effects of prayer on sick patients. Most importantly, the myth doesn't emerge from within a broad range of people who have witnessed the miraculous confirmation of Jesus in their own personal lives.

The stories have been brought together because they belong together. The pressures to keep the stories as separate documents has defeated the understanding of the "Jesus" event as a whole. The miracle of Jesus cannot be seen in a microcosmic vision. It is not important that some pieces of the story might someday need to be altered or proved to be in error. It is far more important that the macrocosm of the story be the less fragile framework for the investigation as a whole.

In addition, the author believes that the rewriting of the various translations into more modern language for the general public is essential to making the information available to the public. This retooling of the language may not be as scholarly and linear as the academics might demand of themselves, but there is a more important strategy in inviting the general public to the "party". The general public is paradoxically the last bastian of objectivity left for Jesus. Maybe that is the way it should have been to begin with. Inviting the general public to the investigation of Jesus, by making the story readable, is ironically the only way to keep the "virus" of the huge hidden agendas from further infecting the earthly understanding of Jesus.

CONCLUSION

It is my hope that your introduction into the childhood of Jesus is interesting and meaningful. You will find a sense of understanding and fulfillment when you encounter them again and again in the varied bibliography. When you stand back and look from a distance, you might see a beauty and harmony that Jesus intended for us all. He is the one that prophesied that someday the things that are hidden will be made known. These stories were meant to be in your hands. They were meant for your family to share and enjoy with all the varied families of the world who have their own stories to tell about Jesus.

When the Indian chief, for example, hears the message from the four corners of the earth, it swells inside him and makes trivial much of what we find important in this life. It takes him out of the world and sits him alongside his ancestors and beside the creator himself. The fraternity of the heavens is a most exquisite sensation—one which allows the "eyes to see" and the "ears to hear" as never before.

Section Two

SMALLER BIBLIOGRAPHY

There are several texts to specifically look for when searching the larger Apocryphal compendiums listed in the Bibliography at the end of this book. These texts contain the majority of the infancy stories used in this work. These seven works are referenced within the story itself. This bibliography is placed in the middle to separate it from the individual published books in the main bibliography and to help the reader with the text as it flows from beginning to end. None of the seven following texts are published separately, so they cannot be referenced in a library like the rest of the bibliography. However, they can be commonly found in a variety of Apocryphal collections like the ones that I have used in the Bibliography.

[a] "THE GOSPEL OF THE BIRTH OF MARY" from the fourth century, often used with works of Jerome, written by Matthew.

[b] The "PROTEVANGELION" or the historical account of the birth of Christ and the perpetual virgin Mary, written by James, considered the first apostle in Jerusalem and the brother of Jesus.

[c] "THE FIRST GOSPEL OF THE INFANCY OF JESUS CHRIST" received by the Gnostics in the second century, used in Africa and Asia as the "only rule of their faith." Mahomet probably used this text in compiling the Koran, often used by early Christians with the other four Gospels, written by Thomas.

[d] "THOMAS' GOSPEL OF THE INFANCY OF JESUS CHRIST" or the "INFANCY GOSPEL NUMBER TWO" thought to have originally been connected to the Gospel of Mary.

[e] The "BIBLE" gospels of Matthew, Mark, Luke and John.

[f] "HISTORY OF JOSEPH, THE CARPENTER, OR DEATH OF JOSEPH" often associated with the above Infancy Gospels.

[g] Extracted from the life of John, according to "SERAPION" often associated with the above Infancy Gospels.

Chapter 7

STORY OF THE
HOLY FAMILY

MARY'S HERITAGE

David, the great-grandfather of Jesus and a descendant of King David, was given a vision that because of his faithfulness he would be the one through whom the prophecy of his fathers would be fulfilled, in that the Redeemer of the world would come out of his family. His wife, Sarah, bore him a son, whom David called Joachim, the grandfather of Jesus. Joachim married his cousin Anna of Bethlehem and together they moved to Nazareth with his flocks and herds which were tended by the shepherds that worked for them. Joachim and Anna were very spiritual people who gave liberally of their earnings to the temple and to the poor and needy. They loved each other very much, but lived childless for about twenty years. Being childless was a great burden to a devout family of those days and a great disappointment to a family who expected the posterity promised to them by an angel. [a, b]

BIRTH OF MARY

Every feast day the Jewish people followed the custom of going to the temple in Jerusalem with friends and neighbors to pray and to celebrate their religious feast days. When the day of the Feast of Dedication approached, Joachim and Anna went to the temple in Jerusalem with some friends to give alms and to pray to the Lord that they might have a child. In their prayers, they promised the Lord that if He would bless them with a child, they would dedicate that child to the service of God. They vowed to send the child in its infancy to serve in the temple, as was the custom for very special children.

When Joachim and Anna arrived at the temple, they met a high priest who was responsible for greeting people at the door. The high priest told Joachim that it was unlawful to offer their alms on that occasion, because Joachim and Anna did not have any children. This was one of the themes for the Feast of Dedication.

Joachim was hurt and ashamed by the words of the priest and left the city. He went into the countryside where he could be alone with his shepherds and where he could fast and pray by himself. Anna returned to their home with their neighbors. After Joachim had fasted and prayed for many days, he was visited by an angel who stood by him in a very bright light. The angel said, "Be not afraid, Joachim. For I am an angel of the Lord, sent to tell you that your prayers are heard and your alms ascend and are accepted in the sight of God. For He surely has seen your shame and heard you unjustly reproached for not having children. God is the avenger of sin and not of nature." The angel then explained that sometimes God does not send people children for a long time so that they may more fully appreciate the gift of a special child. The angel said, "The first mother of your nation was Sarah, the wife of Abraham. Was she not childless in her old age when she had her son Isaac, in whom the promise was fulfilled that a blessing would be given to all nations? Rachel also, so much in favor with God and loved so much by Jacob, continued childless for a long time, yet afterwards was the mother of Joseph, who was not only Governor of Egypt, but delivered many nations from perishing of hunger. Who among the judges was more valiant than Samson, or more holy than Samuel? Yet both their mothers went childless for a long time.

"But if these things will not convince you that I am telling you the truth, then I tell you that Anna, your wife, shall bare you a daughter and you shall call her name Mary. She shall, according to your vow, be devoted to the Lord in the temple from her infancy and be filled with the Holy Ghost from her birth. She shall neither eat nor drink anything which is unclean. Nor shall she converse with the people in the street, but live inside the temple of the Lord. She shall remain inside the temple so that she may not fall under any slander or suspicion. She shall, while yet a virgin, in a way that has never happened before, bring forth a Son of the most High God, who shall be called Jesus. According to the meaning of His name, He shall be the Savior of all nations. This shall be a sign to you of the truthfulness of the things which I am telling you. When you come to the Golden Gate of Jerusalem, you shall meet your wife Anna, who shall rejoice to see you and who has been worried that you did not return sooner."

The angel then departed. The same angel then appeared to Anna, his wife, saying, "Fear not, for I am the angel who has offered up your prayers and alms before God. I am now sent to you to inform you that you will have a baby daughter who shall be called Mary. She shall be blessed above all women. She shall be full of the grace of the Lord. She shall continue during her first three years within her father's house. Afterwards, she shall be taken to the temple to serve the Lord and shall not leave the temple till she arrives at the age of discretion. She shall serve the Lord night and day in fasting and prayer. She shall abstain from every unclean thing and never be with any man while there. But, as a virgin, she shall bring forth a Son, who both by His grace, name and work, shall be the Savior of the world. Arise, therefore, and go up to Jerusalem. As a sign of what I have told you, when you shall come to the place that is called the Golden Gate, you shall meet your husband, who has been concerned for your safety. When you find him waiting for you at the gates, believe that all the rest which I have told you shall also undoubtedly come true."

According to the command of the angel, both Joachim and Anna left the places where they were and went to the gates specified by the angel. They met each other and rejoiced at each other's vision and had great faith in the promise of a child. So Anna conceived and brought forth a daughter and, according to the angel's command, they called her name Mary. [a]

MARY'S YOUTH IN TEMPLE

Mary was born in Nazareth. Joachim and Anna took Mary to Jerusalem at the age of three, as they had promised the Lord, and she walked alone up the fifteen steps of the temple to serve the Lord as a resident of the temple of their fathers. While Mary served in the Temple, Zacharias the priest, who was placed in charge of her keeping, would come into her room and find food and drink that had been brought to her by an angel, and thus it was said that she was fed daily by angels. [a]

BETROTHAL OF MARY

While Mary was in the temple, and well known to be highly favored of God, Abiathar the priest offered many gifts that Mary would marry his son. She refused, saying that she had vowed virginity. When Mary was fourteen, the high priest made a public order that all the virgins in the temple who had come of age should return home. Now that they were grown, they should seek to be married as was the custom in the land.

All the other virgins readily agreed to obey the commands of the high priest. Mary, alone, answered that she could not comply with their commands, saying that both she, and her parents, had promised that she would serve in the temple and that she would remain a virgin. The high priest was troubled, because he could not break the vow that Mary had made. In their scriptures there was a law which said, "Vow and pray." The priest decided that at the approaching feast all the principal people, of both Jerusalem and the surrounding cities should meet and gather their advice collectively on how they should best proceed in this difficult case.

When all the leaders met, they unanimously agreed to ask for the counsel of the Lord on this matter. While they were praying, the High Priest went into the Holy of Holies to consult God. There was a voice from the temple which was heard by all. The voice said that the prophecy of Isaiah about the virgin birth should be consulted. Isaiah had said, "There shall come forth a rod out of the stem of Jesse, and a flower shall spring out of its root, and the Spirit of the Lord shall rest upon him in the form of a dove." The High Priest sent a proclamation to all the men of the house of David who were of marriageable age to bring their rods (the scepter of authority and family leadership) to the altar. He said that out of whosoever's rod grew a flower, and the spirit of God in the form of a dove should light on him, he should be the one chosen to be betrothed to Mary.

Joseph, who was somewhat older than the rest of the suitors, drew back his rod when everyone else presented theirs. When none of the rods presented before the priests sprouted a flower, the High Priest went in and consulted God again. The voice answered the High Priest by saying that the Virgin was to be betrothed to the one person whose rod was not present. Joseph's rod was discovered as the only one missing. When Joseph returned his rod to the temple, his rod sprouted a flower, and a dove flew down and perched upon him. Everyone saw that he was the one to whom the Virgin Mary should be betrothed. There was a ceremony of betrothal and Joseph returned to his own house to prepare for their marriage. Mary returned to her home in Nazareth of Galilee. [a, b]

BIRTH OF JOHN THE BAPTIST

Zacharias, the priest, was married to Elisabeth, the cousin of Mary. Elisabeth and Zacharias had no child and they both were well stricken in years. When Zacharias was administering in the temple, an angel appeared unto Zacharias standing on the right side of the altar of incense. When Zacharias saw the angel, he was frightened and troubled. But the angel said unto him, "Fear not, Zacharias, your prayer has been heard. The prophecy is about to be fulfilled. Your wife Elisabeth shall bear a son and you shall call his name John. He shall go before the Messiah in the spirit and power of Elias, who will come in the spirit and power of your fathers. Your son will be sent to the children and the disobedient to make ready a people prepared for the Lord."

Zacharias said unto the angel, "How shall I know this? I am an old man and my wife well stricken in years."

The angel answering said unto him, "I am Gabriel, who stands in the presence of God. I am sent to speak unto you and to shew you these glad tidings. Behold, you shall be struck dumb and not able to speak until the day when all these things shall be performed, because you have not believed in my words. All these things shall be fulfilled in their own time and season." When Zacharias came out of the temple, he could no longer speak.

When Zacharias beckoned to the people, they saw that he could no longer speak; and they perceived that he had seen a vision in the temple. [e]

Chapter 9

ANNOUNCEMENT
OF THE BIRTH OF JESUS

While Mary was at her home in Nazareth, she also had a visit from Gabriel. Her bedroom chamber was filled with a tremendous light. Amidst the light, Gabriel said, "Hail, Mary! Full of grace. The Lord is with you. You are blessed above all women." But Mary, who had been well acquainted with angels and their light as she worked in the temple, was neither afraid of the vision, nor astonished at the greatness of the light, but only troubled by the words that he spoke. She wondered what a visit from Gabriel meant. Gabriel then said to Mary, "Fear not, Mary. I have not come to cause you to break your vow of chastity, for you have found favor with the Lord. Therefore, while you are yet a Virgin, you shall conceive and bring forth a Son. You shall call His name Jesus. He shall be great. He shall reign from sea to sea and from the rivers to the ends of the earth. He shall be called the Son of the Highest. He who is born on earth reigns exalted in the heavens. The Lord shall give Him the throne of His father David, and He shall reign over the house of Jacob forever, and His kingdom shall have no end. He is the King of Kings and Lord of Lords, and His throne is forever and ever." Mary said, "How can this be? For, in keeping with my vow, I have never been with any man." To this Gabriel replied, "Think not Mary that you shall conceive in the ordinary way. For the Holy Ghost shall come upon you, and the power of the Most High shall overshadow you.

Therefore, He who shall be born of you shall be holy and shall be called the Son of God." Mary then stretched forth her hand and lifted her eyes and said, "Behold the handmaid of the Lord. Let it be unto me according to your word." [a]

MARY'S PREPARATION

After the visit of Gabriel, Mary arose and went into the hill country with haste, into the city of Judah, and entered into the house of Zacharias and saluted Elisabeth. When Elisabeth heard the salutation of Mary, her babe leaped in her womb and Elisabeth was filled with the Holy Ghost. Elisabeth said, "Why has the mother of the Lord come to visit me? As soon as I heard your voice, the babe in my womb leaped for joy." Mary stayed with Elisabeth for about three months. Elisabeth bore her son. When the relatives and neighbors made signs to Zacharias, asking him how he would name his son, he asked for a writing table and wrote saying, "His name is John." At that moment the mouth of Zacharias was opened, his tongue loosed, and he spoke praising God while they all stood in amazement.

Zacharias knew Mary was of the family of David the King and he called her to help weave the veil of the temple while she was at home waiting for Joseph to return. She was chosen from among all the others to weave the true purple for the veil, which was a great honor. Angels administered to Mary in the form of doves while she wove the veil. The doves would light in her window and listen to her sweet voice while she sang, waiting for Joseph to return from building houses abroad. [b]

JOSEPH DISCOVERS MARY WITH CHILD

When her sixth month was come, Joseph returned from his trip building houses, which was his trade. He entered into the house to talk to Mary in a familiar way as one espoused, and he found Mary grown big with child. At the sight of Mary's condition, he struck his face and he said, "With what face can I look up to the Lord my God? What shall I say concerning this young woman? For I received a virgin out of the temple of the Lord my God and have not preserved her that way. Who has deceived me? Who has committed this evil in my house and defiled her? Is this not the history of Adam exactly accomplished in me? For in the very instant of his glory, the serpent came and found Eve alone. After the same manner it has happened to me." Then Joseph, arising from the ground, called her and said, "You who have been so much favored by God, why have you done this? Why have you debased your soul? You were educated in the Holy of Holies and received your food from the hand of angels?" But she, with a flood of tears, replied, "I am innocent and haven't been with any man." Then Joseph said, "Why are you with child?" Mary answered, "As the Lord my God live, I cannot explain it." Then Joseph was greatly afraid and went away to consider what he should do with her.

Joseph thought to himself, "If I conceal her crime, I shall be found guilty of breaking the law of the Lord. I fear that if she is telling the truth and is with child from an angel, I will betray the life of an innocent person to the people." Being a just man, he was not willing to expose her to shame or suspicion. He proposed in his mind to privately dismiss her. While he was meditating on these things, an angel of the Lord appeared to him in private and said, "Joseph, son of David, fear not to take Mary to wife. That which is begotten in her is of the Holy Ghost. She shall have a Son and you shall call His name Jesus. He will be the Savior of the world and save man from his sins." [b]

DISCOVERY OF THE BIRTH AND TRIAL

Annas, a friend of Joseph, came to speak to him and said, "I have not seen you since your return." Joseph replied, "I was weary after my journey and rested the first day." When Annas turned around and saw that Mary was big with child, he left the house of Joseph and went to one of the priests of the temple and told him, "Joseph, in whom you placed so much confidence, is guilty of a notorious crime. He has defiled the virgin, whom he received out of the temple of the Lord and has privately married her and not told anyone." The priest was disturbed at this accusation and asked, "Has Joseph really done this?" Annas replied, "If you send any of your servants to the house of Joseph, you will find that Mary is with child."

The priest sent his servants to see Mary and Joseph and found that Annas was telling the truth. Therefore, Mary and Joseph were brought to trial and the priest said unto her, "Mary, what have you done? Why have you debased your soul and forgotten God? You were raised in the Holy of Holies and you received your food from the hands of angels and heard their songs. Why hast thou done this?" Mary answered in a flood of tears, "As the Lord my God lives, I am innocent in His sight. I have been with no man."

Then the priest said to Joseph, "Why hast thou done this?" Joseph answered, "As the Lord my God lives, I have not been with her." But the priest said, "Do not lie. Tell us the truth. You have privately married her and not told anyone. You should have waited and humbled yourself under the mighty hand of God that you might be blessed." Joseph was silent. Then the priest said, "You must restore to the temple of the Lord the virgin which you took."

Joseph wept bitterly and the priest added, "I will cause you to drink of the water of the Lord, which shall be used as a trial for testing whether you are telling the truth." The priest took the water and made Joseph drink and sent him to a mountainous place. When Joseph returned perfectly well in a few days, all the people wondered why he did not die. The priest then gave to Mary of the Water of the Lord and sent her away. She also returned having no evil come to her. So the priest said, "Since the Lord hath not made your sins evident, neither do I condemn you." So the priest sent them away. Then Joseph took Mary and went to his house rejoicing and praising God. [b]

Chapter 10

JOSEPH'S TRIP
TO BETHLEHEM

And it came to pass, that there was a decree from Caesar Augustus that all the Jews should be taxed. Joseph said, "I will take care that my older children be taxed, but what shall I do with Mary? If I have her taxed as my wife I will be ashamed because she is not yet my wife and if I tax her as my daughter, I will be ashamed because all Israel knows she is not my daughter." He finally decided to leave the matter in the hands of God.

Joseph saddled his donkey and put Mary on it and Joseph and his sons followed after Mary and the donkey to Bethlehem. While traveling, Joseph turned around and saw Mary was sorrowful and said within himself, "Perhaps she is in pain from the child within her." But when he turned about again, he saw her laughing and said to Mary, "Why do I sometimes see you sorrowful and sometimes I see you laughing with joy on your face?" And Mary replied to him, "There are two people inside of me. One is sorrowful with pain and the other is joyful because of the new child to be born." When they were almost to Bethlehem, Mary said to Joseph, "Take me down from the donkey because the child within me is ready to be born." Joseph replied, "Where shall I take you here in this desert?" Mary said again to Joseph, "Take me down, for that which is within me is ready to be born." [b]

BIRTH OF JESUS

Joseph took her down and discovered a cave nearby and he led Mary inside. Joseph left Mary and his sons in the cave and went in haste to seek a Hebrew midwife in the village of Bethlehem. "But as I was going," Joseph said, "I looked up into the air and I saw the clouds appeared strangely and the birds had stopped in the mid air. I looked down toward the earth and saw a table spread and working people sitting around it, but their hands were upon the table and they did not move to eat. Those who had meat in their mouths did not eat it. Those who had lifted their hands up to their heads, did not put their arms down. Those who lifted their hands to their mouths, did not put anything in. All their faces were staring upwards. I saw the sheep had scattered and stood still in the fields. The hand of the shepherd that was lifted to gather the sheep, continued up. I looked toward the river and saw the children, who had gone to take a drink, did not drink.

"Then I saw a woman coming down from the mountains and she said to me, 'Where are you going?' I said to her, 'I am looking for a Hebrew midwife.' She replied to me, 'Where is the woman that is to be delivered?' I answered, 'In the cave, and she is betrothed to me.' Then Solome, the midwife, asked, 'Is she your wife?' I said to her that the mother to be was Mary who was educated in the House of the Lord. I was chosen to be her husband, but she is not yet my wife. She has conceived of God by the power of the Holy Ghost. Solome said, 'Is this true?' and I answered, 'Come and see.'" Solome went along with Joseph and stood in the cave.

A bright cloud overshadowed the cave and Solome said, "This day my soul is magnified, for mine eyes have seen surprising things and salvation is brought to Israel." Just then the cloud became so bright that their eyes could not bear it. When the light gradually decreased, they saw an Infant in the arms of Mary as she was feeding Him. Then Solome cried out and said, "How glorious a day this is? My eyes have seen this extraordinary sight."

Solome had a withered hand. Seeing this, an angel of the Lord stood by Solome and said, "The Lord God hath heard your prayer. Reach forth your hand to the Child and carry him and by doing so your hand shall be restored." Solome, filled with joy, went to the Child and said, "Let me touch Him." When she picked up the Baby Jesus she had the intention of worshiping Him and she said, "This is a great King which is born in Israel." Solome was made whole from that moment. A voice came to Solome, "Do not talk about these strange things which you have seen until the Child returns to Jerusalem." [b]

BABY JESUS BROUGHT TO TEMPLE

Jesus was presented before the temple of the Lord with offerings, according to the requirement of the law of Moses. The law said that every first born male shall be set apart as holy. When the old priest Simeon, who later took the place of Zacharias, saw Jesus shining as a pillar of light in the arms of Mary, he was filled with the greatest pleasure. Angels stood around the Baby Jesus, adoring him as the guards would for a king. Then Simeon went near to Mary and stretched forth his hands toward the Baby and said, "Now, O my Lord, I shall die in peace, according to the promise which has been made to me. For mine eyes have seen the vessel of the salvation of all nations...a light to all people and the glory of Israel." [c]

THE WISE MEN

When Joseph was preparing to go home to Nazareth, there arose a great commotion in Bethlehem. Wise Men had come from the east and asked, "Where has the King of the Jews been born? We have seen His star in the east and are come to worship him." When Herod heard this, he was worried for his own throne and sent a messenger to these foreign kings and to the priests of the temple to ask them where to find this Baby King. The servant of Herod asked the priests of the temple in the town hall, "Where are your writings concerning Christ the King telling us where He should be born?" The priests said unto the servant of Herod, "It is written that the Baby is to be born in Bethlehem. He shall be the greatest of the Princes of Judah and shall become a Ruler of the people of Israel."

When the servant of Herod had sent the priests of the temple away, he asked the Wise Men in the town hall, "What sign were you told to look for at the coming of the Baby King and what sign did you see?" They answered him, "We saw a large star shining among the stars of heaven and it so outshined all the other stars, that it made the stars around it no longer visible. We therefore knew that the great King was born in Israel and have come to worship him." Herod sent the Wise Men a message to find the Baby King and bring him word so that he might worship Him also. So the Wise Men followed the star to where the Baby Jesus was with His Mother. They brought out their treasures and offered them to the Baby Jesus—gold, frankincense and myrrh. Then Mary took one of His swaddling clothes, in which she had wrapped the Baby Jesus, and gave it to them instead of a blessing, which they received as a most noble present. That night, the Wise Men were warned in a dream by an angel that they should not return to Herod. So they departed into their own country another way. [b]

MISTAKE THAT COST
THE LIFE OF ZACHARIAS

When Herod learned that he was mocked by the Wise Men, he was very angry and commanded certain men to go and to kill all the children who were in Bethlehem and the regions round about from two years old and under. However, an angel of the Lord appeared to Joseph in his sleep and said, "Arise, take the Child and His mother and go into Egypt as soon as the cock crows." Joseph arose in the early morning light and took his family south towards Egypt.

Elisabeth, the mother of the newly born John the Baptist, also heard about Herod's intentions to kill all the babies of the city and surrounding lands and knew that her son John was in danger. She hurried and took John and went into the mountains and looked around for a place to hide him. There was no secret place to be found. Then she groaned within herself and said, "O mountain of the Lord, receive the mother with the child." Elisabeth was old and could not climb the steepness of the mountain. Instantly the mountain was divided and she was able to climb up. An angel of the Lord appeared to Elisabeth and her baby to protect them.

Herod made a great search for the baby John and sent servants to Zacharias, when he was ministering at the altar, and said to him, "Where have you hid your son?" He replied to them, "I am a minister of God and a servant at the altar. How should I know where my son is?" So the servants went back and told Herod everything. He was angry and said, "Is not Zacharias' son the one most likely to be this King in Israel?" Herod sent his servants again to Zacharias saying, "Tell us the truth. Where is your son? For you know that your life is in our hands." But Zacharias replied to them, "I am a martyr for God and if Herod shed my blood, the Lord will receive my soul. Let it be known that you shed innocent blood."

Zacharias was murdered between the entrance of the temple and the altar. However, the people did not know when Zacharias was killed. When the priests returned to the temple, they expected Zacharias to greet and bless them. However, Zacharias did not come out to meet them at the entrance of the temple, as was the custom. They waited for him for a long time and still he did not come. One of them ventured into the holy place where the altar was and he saw blood lying on the ground. A voice from heaven said, "Zacharias is murdered and his blood shall not be wiped away until the revenger of his blood is come."

When the priest heard this, he was afraid and went and told the others what he had seen and heard. They all went in and saw the fact. Then the roofs of the temple began to howl and the veils of the temple were rent from the top to the bottom. However, they could not find the body, only the blood, a part of which had been made hard as stone. The priests went away and told all the people that Zacharias was murdered. The tribes of Israel mourned for him three days. Some of the blood of Zacharias was carried to the mountain and spilled on a rock in fulfillment of the prophecy of Ezekiel (Ezekiel 24: 6-8) that God would take vengeance on those that killed the priests and the children. When the frightened Herod heard these things, he also shed the blood of animals, small boys and even many priests in an attempt to cover the stain in the temple, but the stain remained unchanged. [b]

SUCCESSOR FOR ZACHARIAS

The priests took counsel together concerning a person to succeed Zacharias. Simeon and the other priests cast lots and the lot fell upon Simeon. Simeon had been assured by the Holy Spirit that he should not die until he had seen Christ come in the flesh. This he had already seen when Mary came to observe the law of purification and the ordinance of redemption in behalf of her firstborn Son (Ex 13: 2-13, Num 18: 15). [b]

Chapter 11

HOLY FAMILY MIGRATES TO EGYPT

Joseph and his family were going to Egypt when the girts of the saddle broke. They came near to a great city in which there was an idol to which the people brought their offerings and other offerings from their other gods and idols. Beside this idol stood a priest who ministered to it, who, as often as Satan spoke out of the idol, related the things the idol said to the inhabitants of Egypt. This priest had a son who was possessed with a great number of evil spirits. He uttered many strange things when the devils seized him. He walked about naked with his clothes torn, throwing stones at those whom he saw.

Near the idol was the inn of the city in which Joseph and his family planned to stay. There was a great commotion in the idols of the city and all the inhabitants of the city were astonished. The magistrates and priests of the idols assembled before their principal idol and they asked that idol, "What is this great disturbance in our country?" The idol answered them, "The unknown God is come, who is truly God. There is no one besides him who is worthy of divine worship. He is truly the Son of God." When the idol had said this, the fame of the Baby Jesus spread among the people and they began to tremble. The idol then said, "We ourselves are afraid by the greatness of His power." At the same instant the idol fell down, and at its fall all the inhabitants of Egypt ran together.

However, the son of the priest, when his usual disorder came upon him, went into the inn and found Joseph and Mary, whom all the rest had left behind. When Mary had washed the swaddling clothes of the Baby Jesus, she had hung them out to dry upon a post. The boy, possessed with the devil, took one of them down and put it on his head. Presently, the devils began to come out of him. From that time the boy was healed by the power of the Lord and he began to sing praises and give thanks to the Lord who had healed him. When his father saw him restored to his former state of health, he said, "My son, what has happened to you? By what means are you cured?" The boy answered, "When the devils seized me, I went into the inn and found a very handsome woman with a boy, whose swaddling clothes she had just washed and hung out upon a post to dry. I took one of them and put it upon my head and immediately the devils left me and fled away." At this the father rejoiced and said, "My son, perhaps this Baby is the Son of the living God who made the heavens and the earth. For as soon as He came amongst us, the idol where I stood to administer was broken. All the gods fell down and were destroyed by a greater power." Therefore, the prophecy was fulfilled which said, "Out of Egypt I have called my Son." [c]

DESTRUCTION OF IDOLS

Now when Joseph and Mary heard that the idol had fallen down and was destroyed, they were very much afraid and said, "When we were in the land of Israel, Herod, intending to kill Jesus, slew all the infants at Bethlehem. There is no doubt that when the Egyptians hear that this idol has broken and fallen down, they will burn us with fire." They went, therefore, to the secret places of thieves who robbed travelers of their carriages and their clothes as they passed by, and carried the travelers away bound. These thieves heard a great noise as Joseph and his family approached. The noise they heard was like a king with a great army riding many horses. They heard trumpets sounding as if this king were departing from his own city. The robbers were so afraid that they fled, leaving all their booty behind them. When this happened, all the prisoners arose and loosed each other's bonds, and each man who was a prisoner took his bags and began to run away when they saw Joseph and Mary coming towards them. The prisoners asked, "Where is that King, the noise of whose approach the robbers heard and caused them to flee and to leave us safe?" Joseph answered, "He will come after us." [c]

BABY JESUS HEALS WOMAN

Then they went into another city where there was a woman possessed with a devil, in whom Satan resided. One night, when she went to fetch water, she could no longer endure her clothes, nor to be in any house. As often as the people would tie her with chains or cords, she would break them and go out into the desert places, sometimes standing where roads crossed and in churchyards and would throw stones at men. When Mary saw this woman, she pitied her. Whereupon, Satan presently left her and fled away saying, "Woe to me because of Mary and her Son." So the woman was delivered from her torment. When the woman was healed, she found herself naked and blushed and avoided seeing any man until she could put her clothes on. When she went home, she gave an account of her case to her father and her family. As they were the most affluent family of the city, they entertained Mary and Joseph with the greatest respect. [c]

BABY JESUS HEALS THE BRIDE

The next morning, having received a sufficient supply of provisions for the road, the Holy Family left. About evening time they arrived at another town where a marriage was about to be solemnized, but the bride was deaf and without speech. When the bride saw Mary entering into the town and carrying Jesus in her arms, she stretched out her hands to the Baby and took him in her arms and hugged and kissed him, while continually moving him and pressing him to her body. Suddenly the string of her tongue was loosed and her ears were opened and she began to sing praises to God who had restored her. There was a great joy among the inhabitants of the town that night. They thought that God and His angels had come down among them. The Holy Family stayed in this place for three days, being met with the greatest respect and most splendid of entertainment. [c]

BATH WATER FROM JESUS HEALS LEPER

The next day a woman brought perfumed water to wash the Baby Jesus. When she had washed Jesus, she preserved the water. There was a girl in the town whose body was white with leprosy. The woman, who had bathed Jesus, took some of the water and sprinkled it on the girl and she was cleansed from her leprosy. The people said, "Without a doubt Joseph and Mary and the Boy are gods." [c]

SON OF THE PRINCE OF EGYPT HEALED

When they were making ready to go, the girl, who had been troubled with the leprosy, came and desired they would permit her to go along. They consented, and the girl went with them to another city where there was a palace of a great King whose house was not far from the inn. Here they stayed. The girl went out the next day and met the Prince's wife and found her in a sorrowful state. The girl asked the Prince's wife the reason for her tears. She replied, "Wonder not at my groans, for I am under such a great misfortune that I dare not tell anyone." But the girl said, "If you will entrust me with your private grievance, perhaps I may find you a remedy for it."

The Prince's wife said, "I have been married to the Prince who rules as King over large dominions. I lived a long time with him before we had a child. At last I bore a child, but he was born leprous. When the prince saw the baby, he said to me, 'Either you

76

kill the baby or send him to some nurse in such a place that he may never be heard of.' Take care of yourself, for I will never see you again. So here I pine," said the Prince's wife. The young girl replied, "I have found a remedy for your baby's disease, I promise you. For I also was leprous, but God cleansed me, even He who is called Jesus, the Son of Mary." The prince's wife asked, "Where is the Child and His mother of whom you have spoken? By what means are you cured?" The girl said, "I took the water with which His body had been washed and poured it upon me and my leprosy went away."

The Prince's wife then arose and entertained Joseph and Mary, providing a great feast among a large company of men. The next day she took perfumed water to wash Jesus and afterwards poured the water upon her son, whom she had brought with her. Her son was instantly cleansed from his leprosy. She began to sing thanks and praises unto God and said, "Blessed is the mother that bare thee, O Jesus." She then offered very large gifts to Mary and sent them on their way, with all imaginable respect. [c]

HOLY FAMILY OBTAINS HELP FROM ROBBERS

In their journey, they came to a desert infested with robbers, so Joseph and Mary prepared to pass through it at night. When they were going along, they saw two robbers in the road and a great number of other robbers, who were their companions. All of the robbers were lying down as if they were asleep. The names of these two were Titus and Dumachus. Titus took compassion on the family of Joseph with their Baby and said to Dumachus, "Let these people pass along quietly so that our friends will not know that they are here." But Dumachus refused and Titus turned and said, "I will give you forty goats if you let these people pass and, as a pledge, take my girdle." Titus gave Dumachus the girdle before he finished speaking so that Dumachus might not open his mouth or make a noise.

When Mary saw the kindness which this robber showed them, she said to Titus, "May the Lord God receive you to His right hand and grant thee pardon for your sins." The Baby Jesus answered and said to His mother, "When thirty years are expired, Mother, the Jews will crucify me at Jerusalem. These two thieves shall be with me at the same time upon the cross, Titus on my right hand and Dumachus on my left. At that time Titus shall go before me into paradise." When Jesus had said these things, His mother said, "God forbid that this should happen to my Son." [c]

HOLY FAMILY RETURNS TO JUDEA

They went to the place with the sycamore tree, which is now called Matarea. In Matarea, Jesus caused a well to spring forth in which Mary washed His coat. Then they proceeded to Memphis and saw Pharaoh and they abode in Egypt. The Lord Jesus did very many miracles in Egypt which are not found. At the end of their stay, the Holy Family returned to Judea, but Joseph was afraid to enter, hearing that Archelaus, the son of Herod, was made the new King. An angel of the lord appeared to Joseph and told him, "Fear not to go to Nazareth and live there."

Mary used to take hold of Jesus' hand and lead him along the roads, saying, "My sweet Son, walk a little way" the same manner as all other babes are taught to walk. Jesus followed after her untroubled. He clung to her with His little fingers. He stopped from time to time and He hung on to the skirts of Mary. He would lift up His eyes to her face and she would catch Him up to herself and lift Him up in her arms and walk along with Him. [c]

BABY JESUS CURES DISTEMPER

When they came to the city Bethlehem, they found several very desperate types of distemper, which became so troublesome to children that most of them died. There was a woman who brought her son, who was at the point of death, to Mary, who was bathing the Baby Jesus. The woman said, "O Mary, look down upon this my son who is afflicted with most dreadful pains." Mary, hearing her said, "Take a little of this water with which I have washed my Son and sprinkle it upon him." Then she took a little of the water, as Mary had commanded, and sprinkled it upon her son, who tired in his pain and had fallen asleep. After he had slept a little, he awoke perfectly well. The mother was abundantly glad and went again to Mary. Mary said to her, "Give praise to God, who hath cured your son." [c]

BARTHOLOMEW CURED IN BED OF JESUS

Another woman in that city had two sick sons. When one of them had died, the other at the point of death, she took him in her arms to Mary and in a flood of tears said, "Mary, relieve me. For I had two sons, one of which I have just now buried. The other I see is just at the point of death. I seek a favor from God, O gracious and merciful Lord. Thou hast given me two sons. One of them you have taken to yourself. Spare me the other." Mary perceived the greatness of her sorrow and with pity said, "Place your son in my Son's bed and cover him with His clothes." She placed him in the bed where the Baby Jesus had lain at the moment when his eyes were just closed by death, and as soon as he touched the bedding of the Baby Jesus, his eyes were opened. The baby called out with a loud voice to his mother. He asked for bread. Then his mother said, "Mary, now I am assured that the powers of God do dwell in you and that your Son can cure children who are like himself." The boy who was cured was Bartholomew mentioned in the Gospels. [c]

MIRACLE IN DYE SHOP

Mary went to a neighbor's house, whose profession was a dyer of cloth. Jesus went with her, as is the want of all children to follow their mothers. Now while Mary spoke to the master of the shop, Jesus went into the place where the man kept his vessels of several colors of dye. Beside the vessels were the cloths that

79

people had brought to be colored. Jesus wrapped all the cloths together and sunk them into the vessel that contained black dye. When the master of the shop saw what Jesus had done, he became angry and began to complain to Mary saying, "Look what your Son has done. He has destroyed my work. This child shall not leave my shop until all the damage which He has done is made good." Hearing the words of the man, Mary, being confused, looked at her Son and said, "My beloved Son, what have you done? You have always brought me great joy and now you have made me sad." The child Jesus answered His mother and said, "How have I made you sad?" Mary replied, "Look at all the damage you have caused. The cloths were to be of several colors and you made them all one color. Now I must pay for what you have done." Jesus looked at His mother and the master of the shop and walked over to the vessel of black dye and started to pull out the cloths which were no longer of one color. They were of many colors, as they were intended to be. When Jesus handed the cloths to the shopkeeper, both he and Mary marveled at what Jesus had done. As the man praised him, Mary took Jesus in her arms and kissed him. Mary was filled with great joy and returned to her house with Christ, her Son. [c]

JESUS PLAYS WITH JUDAS

Another woman had a son who was possessed by Satan. This boy was named Judas. As often as Satan seized him, he was inclined to bite all that were present. If he found no one else near him, he would bite his own hands and other parts. But the mother of this miserable boy, hearing of Mary and her Son, Jesus, arose and brought her son to Mary. In the meantime, James and Joses had taken Jesus to play with the other children. Judas, who was possessed, came and sat down at the right hand of Jesus. When Satan had overcome him, in his usual fashion, Judas went about to bite the Child Jesus. The child Judas tried but he could not do it, so he struck Jesus on the right side so that he cried out. In that same moment, Satan went out of Judas. This same boy, who struck Jesus, and out of whom Satan went, was Judas Iscariot, who betrayed Jesus to the Jews. That same side, on which Judas struck him, the Roman soldiers pierced with a spear. [c]

JESUS HELPS CORRECT KING'S THRONE

There came a time when the King of Jerusalem sent for Joseph and said, "I would have you make me a throne to occupy the place where I commonly sit." Joseph obeyed and began the work. He continued two years in the King's palace before he finished it. When Joseph and Jesus came to put the throne in its place, Joseph found it wanted two spans on each side of the appointed measure. When the King saw what had happened, he was very angry with Joseph. Joseph, afraid of the King's anger, went to bed without his supper, taking nothing to eat. Then Jesus asked him, "What are you afraid of?" Joseph replied, "I am afraid that I have lost my labor in the work which I have been about these two years." Jesus said, "Do not be afraid or sad. Lay hold on one side of the throne and I will take hold of the other and we will bring it to its just dimensions." When Joseph had done as Jesus said, each of them with all their strength pulled on his side. The throne obeyed and was brought to the proper dimensions of the place. When they who stood by saw this miracle, they were astonished and praised God. The throne was made of the same fine cedar wood which grew in Solomon's time, and it was adorned with various shapes and figures. [c]

JESUS HEALS BOY'S FOOT

There was a boy in the village of Nazareth who was chopping wood when he struck his foot with the blade. Many of the townspeople rushed to his side. Jesus was among them. He knelt down by the boy and put His hands on the injured foot. The foot was healed while the villagers looked on. Jesus said to the boy, "Arise, return to your work, and as you do so, remember me." When the crowd saw what Jesus had done they worshiped him and said, "We believe that you are the Son of God." [c]

81

JESUS HEALS SIMON THE CANAANITE

Jesus gathered together the boys in His play and ranked them as though He were a King. The boys spread their garments on the ground for Jesus to sit on. Having made a crown of flowers, they put it upon His head and stood on His right and left as the guards of a King. If anyone happened to pass by, they took them and said, "Come and worship the King, that you may have a prosperous journey."

In the meantime, while these things were happening, there came certain men carrying a boy upon a couch. This boy, having gone with his companions to the mountain to gather wood, found a partridge's nest. The boy put his hand into the nest to take out the eggs and was bitten by a poisonous serpent which leaped out of the nest. The boy then cried out for the help of his companions. When his companions came, they found him lying upon the earth like a dead person.

The neighbors of the boy carried him back into the city on a couch. When they came to the place where Jesus was sitting like a King, the boy guards ran to bring those who carried the couch and bid them pay their respects to the King. Those who carried the couch were too sorrowful and they refused to come. The boys drew them and forced them against their will to come. When they passed Jesus, he inquired what had happened to the boy on the couch. They answered that a serpent had bitten him. Jesus said to the boys, "Let us go and kill that serpent." The parents of the boy desired to be excused because their son lay at the point of death. When they heard the parents refuse, the friends of Jesus said, "Did you not hear what the King said? Let us go and kill the serpent." So they brought the couch back again to the place of the serpent even though they didn't want to.

When they came to the nest, Jesus said to the boys, "Is this the serpent's lurking place?" They said, "It is." Then Jesus called to the serpent to come forth and it came out of its hiding place. Jesus said to the serpent, "Go and suck out all the poison which you have infused into that boy." So the serpent crept to the boy and took away all its poison. Jesus then touched the boy and restored him to health. When the boy began to cry, Jesus said, "Cease crying, for hereafter thou shalt be my disciple." This was that Simon the Canaanite, who is mentioned in the Gospel. [c]

JESUS HEALS HIS BROTHER JAMES

On another day Joseph sent his son James to gather wood with Jesus. When they came to the place where there was wood, James began to gather it. Suddenly a venomous viper bit him, so that he began to cry. Jesus, seeing him in this condition, came and blew upon the place where the viper had bit him and it was instantly well. [c]

JESUS RAISES FRIEND FROM DEATH

On a certain day, Jesus was with some boys who were playing on the housetop and one of the boys fell down and presently died. All the other boys ran away. Jesus alone was left on the housetop. When the family of the dead boy came, they said to Jesus, "You threw our son down from the housetop." Jesus denied to them that He had done what they had accused him of. Then the family of the boy cried out, "Our son is dead and this is he who killed him."

Jesus replied to them, "Do not charge me with a crime of which you are not able to convict me. Let us go ask the boy himself. He will tell us the truth." Jesus went down and stood over the head of the dead boy and said with a loud voice, "Zeinunus, who threw you down from the housetop?"

Then the dead boy answered, "You did not throw me down, but someone else did." When Jesus bade those who stood by to take notice of the risen boy's words, all who were present praised God. [c]

JESUS RETRIEVES SPILT WATER

One time Mary had commanded that Jesus fetch her some water out of the well. When He had gone to fetch the water, the pitcher broke. But Jesus, spreading His mantle on the ground, gathered up the water again in His cloak and brought it to His mother. She was astonished at this thing. [c]

JESUS MAKES CLAY BIRDS FLY

Again, on another day, Jesus was with some boys by a river and they drew water out of the river by little channels and made little pools. Jesus made twelve sparrows out of clay from the banks on the little pools and placed them round about, three on a side. However, it was the Sabbath day and the son of Hanani, a Jew, came by and saw them making these things and said, "Why do you make figures of clay on the Sabbath?" Then the son of Hanani ran as if to destroy their pools. Jesus, seeing what was about to happen, clapped His hands over the sparrows which He had made and they fled away chirping. At length the son of Hanani destroyed the pools and the water vanished away. Jesus said to him, "What have these pools done to you?" [c, d]

JESUS AND MARY IN WILDERNESS TO HELP JOHN THE BAPTIST

When Elisabeth passed away, John the Baptist sat weeping over her. He did not know how to shroud her and bury her, because on the day of her death he was only seven years old.

Jesus, who could see the heavens and earth, saw His kinsman John sitting and weeping near His mother. He began to weep for a long time, although no one knew the cause of His weeping. When Mary saw Jesus weeping, she said to him, "Why are you weeping? Did Joseph or someone else chide you?" Jesus answered, "No, mother, the real reason is that your kinswoman, the old Elisabeth, has left my beloved John an orphan. He is now weeping over her body, which is lying in the mountain."

When Mary heard this, she began to weep over her kinswoman. Jesus said to her, "Do not weep mother. We will go to see her in this very hour. Call Solome and let us take her with us." They went to the wilderness to the spot where the body of Elisabeth lay and where John was sitting. When John heard them coming, he was frightened and left the body of his mother. A voice reached him immediately and said to him, "Do not be afraid, John. I am your kinsman Jesus and I have come with my mother in order to attend to the business of the burial of Elisabeth, your happy mother, because she is my mother's kinswoman." When John heard this, he turned back to Christ and His mother and embraced them. Then the Savior said to His mother, "Arise, Mother and Solome, and wash the body." They washed the body of Elisabeth in the spring from which she would draw water for herself and her son. Then Mary held John and wept over him and cursed Herod for the numerous crimes which he had committed.

Then the angels, Michael and Gabriel, came down from heaven and dug a grave and the Savior said to them, "Go and bring the soul of Zacharias and of the priest, Simeon, in order that they may sing while you bury the body." Michael brought immediately the soul of Zacharias and Simeon, who shrouded the body of Elisabeth and sang for a long time. Jesus and his mother stayed near John seven days and consoled him at the death of his mother and taught him how to live in the desert.

Then Jesus said to His mother, "Let us go to the place where I may proceed with my work." Then Mary wept immediately over the loneliness of John, who was very young, and said, "We will take him with us since he is an orphan without anyone." Then Jesus said to her, "This is not the will of my Father who is in the heavens. He shall remain in the wilderness until the day of his showing unto Israel. Instead of a desert full of wild beasts, he will walk in a desert full of angels and prophets, as if there were multitudes of people. Here is also Gabriel, the head of the angels, whom I have appointed to protect him and to grant to him power from heaven. Further, I shall render the water of this spring as sweet and delicious to him as mother's milk. There is no mother who loves him more in all the world. Zacharias also loves him, and I have ordered him to come and inquire after John, because although his body is buried in the earth, his soul is alive."

These words Christ spoke to His mother while John was in the desert. When John looked at them as they departed, he wept. Mary wept bitterly over John saying, "Woe is me, John, because you are alone in the desert without anyone. Where is Zacharias, your father, and where is Elisabeth, your mother? Let them come and weep with me today." Jesus said to her, "Do not weep over this child, mother. I shall not forget him." [g]

JESUS BEGINS HIS SCHOOLING

There was also at Jerusalem one named Zaccheus, who was a schoolmaster. He said to Joseph, "Joseph, why don't you send Jesus to me that I may teach him His letters?" Joseph agreed and told Mary. So they brought him to that master who, as soon as he saw Jesus, wrote out an alphabet for him. The teacher asked Jesus to say Aleph. When Jesus had said Aleph, the master asked him to pronounce Beth. Then Jesus said to him, "Tell me first the meaning of the letter Aleph and then I will pronounce Beth." When the master threatened to whip him, Jesus explained to him the meaning of the letters Aleph and Beth. Jesus also showed the master which letters had straight figures and which were oblique and what letters had double figures and which had points and which had none. Jesus went on to explain why one letter went before another and many other things He began to tell Zaccheus and explain, which the master himself had never heard nor read in any book. Jesus further said to the master, "Take notice how I say them." Then He began clearly and distinctly to say Aleph, Beth, Gimel, Daleth, and so on to the end of the alphabet. At this, the master was so surprised that he said, "I believe this boy was born before Noah." Turning to Joseph, the master said, "You have brought a boy to me to be taught who is more learned than any master." Then he also said to Mary, "This, your Son, has no need of learning." [c]

86

JESUS TEACHES AT THE TEMPLE

When Jesus was twelve years old, Mary and Joseph brought him to Jerusalem to the feast of the Passover. When the feast was over, they began to return to their home. But Jesus continued behind in the temple among the doctors and elders and learned men of Israel, to whom Jesus proposed several questions of learning. He also gave them answers. He said to them, "Whose Son is the Messiah?" They answered, "The Son of David." "Why then," said He, "does He call on the name of the Lord? And the Lord said to him, 'Sit at my right hand till I have made your enemies your footstool'."

Then a certain principal Rabbi asked him, "Have you read books?" Jesus answered and said that He had read books. Jesus then explained to them the books of the law and precepts and statutes and the mysteries which are contained in the books of the prophets—things which the mind of no creature could reach. Then the Rabbi said, "I never yet have seen or heard of such knowledge! What do you think that boy will be?" All that heard him were astonished at His understanding and His answers.

A certain astronomer, who was present, asked Jesus whether He had studied astronomy. Jesus answered and told him the number of the spheres and heavenly bodies, also their triangular, square and sectile aspect, their progressive and retrograde motion, their size and several prognostications and other things which the reason of man had never discovered.

There was also among them a philosopher well skilled in physics and natural philosophy who asked Jesus whether He had studied physics and metaphysics. Jesus explained to him physics and metaphysics, also those things which were above and below the power of nature. Jesus explained the powers of the body, its humors and their effects. He also explained the number of the members of the body and the bones, veins, arteries, and nerves, the several constitutions of body, hot and dry, cold and moist, and the tendencies of them, how the soul operated upon the body, what its various sensations and faculties were, the faculty of speaking, anger, desire, and lastly the manner of its composition and dissolution. Jesus also explained other things which the understanding of no other creature had ever reached. Then the philosopher arose and worshiped Jesus and said, "O Lord Jesus, from henceforth I will be your disciple and servant."

While they were discoursing on these things, Mary came in, having been three days walking about with Joseph seeking for Jesus. When she saw Jesus sitting among the doctors, and in His turn proposing questions to them and giving answers, she said to Jesus, "My Son, why have you done thus to us? Behold, your father and I have been worried and have been looking for you."

Jesus replied, "Why were you looking for me? Didn't you know that I ought to be about my father's business?" But they didn't understand the words which He said to them. Then the doctors asked Mary if Jesus was her Son. When she said He was, they said, "O happy Mary, who has given birth to such a Son." Then Jesus returned with Joseph and Mary to Nazareth and obeyed them in all things. [c]

JESUS IS BAPTIZED BY JOHN THE BAPTIST

Now from this time Jesus began to conceal His miracles and secret works. He gave himself to the study of the law till He arrived to the end of His thirtieth year. At that time He was baptized by John the Baptist and the Lord of Heavens publicly owned him at the Jordan River, sending down this voice from heaven, "This is my beloved Son in whom I am well pleased." The Holy Ghost was also present in the form of a dove. [c]

DEATH OF JOSEPH

When Joseph became ill, he went to the temple to pray to be delivered from the terrors of death. When he got home, he fell ill and weak. Jesus said, "I wept. My mother asked if Joseph must die and I told her that it must be so. I sat at his head, Mary at his feet. Mary felt his feet and legs and found them cold as ice. My brothers and sisters were summoned. Lysia, my oldest sister, lamented. So did all. I looked at the south of the door and saw the angel appointed to take him at his death and other angels. Joseph saw them and feared. I rebuked them and the angels fled, except the one who was behind the door. I prayed for protection for the soul of Joseph. When I had said Amen, my mother answered me, in the language of the inhabitants of the heavens of Michael and of Gabriel. The choir of the angels came. Numbness and panting seized Joseph. The angel, appointed to take him at his death, was timid. I arose and went outside and bade him go in and do his appointed work. Joseph died at sunrise.

"The people of Nazareth came and mourned till the ninth hour. Then I put all forth, anointed and washed the body, angels came and shrouded the body, and the body was laid beside Jacob, his father."

The apostles later asked why Joseph should not have been exempted from death like Enoch and Elias. Jesus said that death was inevitable and then said that both Enoch and Elias will have to die as well and are in trouble until their death is over. At the end of the world the Antichrist will shed the blood of two men, because of the reproaches the two men will heap upon him. The apostles asked, "Who are these two men?" Jesus answered and said, "Enoch and Elias". [f]

Chapter 12

OVERVIEW OF THE
BIBLIOGRAPHY

The original texts may shock the readers on a number of levels. They may sound foreign and complex because they are written by people so long ago. Most of them have not been rewritten, as this work has been, to make them as readable as the Bible. Reading the Bible itself can be a challenge for the lay reader. However, the Bible has the advantage of hundreds of years of clarification by experts. The second shock for the more adventurous will be how much material is not included in the Bible. That one speaks for itself.

The last and most important shock to the beginning reader of the original texts, is that they contain ideas, people and concepts that are totally without contemporary reference. Without a road map and a travel guide, parts of them may not make the slightest sense, much like reading the Book of Revelation for the first time. The original texts can offend, inspire, convince, provoke, enlighten and confuse all at the same time. Some of them can even make you laugh. The magic of these documents is that when they begin to come together in one's mind, a most miraculous picture begins to emerge. Jesus becomes the Savior of the world and not just the reason for a church from Judea.

There will arise a bizarre story or two surrounding the life of the Savior, which is just too much for us to swallow if we are to take it literally. For example, in one story Jesus slides down a beam of light. Is it possible that someone seeing Christ in one of his heavenly communications, might describe what they saw in just such a confusing way? Every "people" have their colloquialisms.

Do not get discouraged or feel ignorant. Begin by taking the more readable sections and enjoy the new insights as they come. When you follow the trails that link documents together, they lead to places few men have ever gone. Reserve your judgments on the ideas that are different from yours until you have cross-read them from different directions. They will make more sense that way. Remember one startling fact, Jesus didn't write any of them, nor the Bible for that matter. The writers, his friends and apostles, were fishermen, tax collectors, carpenters and a variety of different professions. Few were professional historians or writers. Most of them were not well educated and used scribes to record for them.

Ask the guys that built your house or farmed your food to write your story and see how clear it is; then ask some guy whom you never met to translate your story into a different language a couple of times; record them on biodegradable leather, or primitive parchments; bury them for two thousand years; and hope that your distant posterity won't hate you for leaving them with that mess. Maybe a very few would pick up the documents and make sense of them and really get to know important things about you.

The question of divine origin and the inspiration of the writers may elude you at first; however, the message becomes poignantly clear with time and effort. It will emerge for the very persistent like a phoenix out of a funeral pyre and may demand something from you that may change your life. That is the most frightening idea of all.

BIBLIOGRAPHY

(1) Abdullah Yusuf Ali, The Holy Qur'an

(2) Analecta Bollandiana

(3) Acta apostolorum Apocrcrypha I, ed. Lipisius, 1891; II 1 and 2 ed

(4) Aland, K., Neue Neutestamentliche Papyri II, 1965/66

(5) Apostelgeschichten (Apocryphal Acts)

(6) Aufstieg und Niedrgang der Rômishchen Welt

(7) Barnstone, W., The Other Bible, 1984

(8) Bibliotheca hagiographica Graeca 1957

(9) Bibliotheca hagiographica Latina, 1949

(10) Bibliotheca hagiographica orientalis, 1910

(11) Bonnet, 1898 and 1903 (reprint 1959)

(12) Bromiley, G.W., Theological Dictionary of the New Testament, tr.
    (ET of Theologisches Wôrterbuch zum NT, 1933)

(13) Corpus Christianorum, Series Latina, 1953ff.

(14) Corpus Christianorum, Series Graeca, 1976ff.

(15) Corpus Christianorum, Series Apocryphorum, 1983ff.

(16) Corpus scriptorum Christianorum orientalium

(17) Corpus scriptorum ecclesiasticorum Latinorum, Vienna

(18) Dictionnaire d'archeologie chretienne it de liturgie

(19) Dunstan, Victor, Did the Virgin Mary Live and Die in England? 1985

(20) Elder, I. Hill, Celt, Druid and Culdee

(21) Elliott, Remarkable Characters and Places in the Holy Land

(22) Gaster, Theodor H., The Dead Sea Scriptures, 1976

(23) Gayer, The Heritage of the Anglo-Saxon Race

(24) Gli, Mario Erbetta, Apocrifi del Nuovo Testament, I-III, 1966-81

(25) Goodsspeed, E. J., The Story of the Apocrypha, 1939

(26) Gordon, E. O., Prehistoric London

(27) Gôttinger Theologische Arbeiten 1975ff.

(28) G. Graf, Geschichte der christlichen arabishcen Literatur, 1-5, 1944-1953

(29) Grundkurs Theologie, Stuttgart 1989ff.

(30) Hansen, L. Taylor, He Walked the Americas, 1963

(31) Harnack, Adolf, Geshichte der altchristlichen Literatur bis Eusebius, 1958

(32) Heath Alban, The Painted Savages of England

(33) Hennecke, Edgar, Neuetestamentliche Apokrphen in deutscher Ûberzetzund, ed., 1904
id., 2nd edition, 1924
id., 3rd edition, ed. E. Hennecke and W. Schneemelcher 1959/1964 (reprint 1968; ET 1963, 1965; 2nd impression 1973,1974)

(34) Holladay, W. L., Journal of Biblical Literature, 1972

(35) James, M.R., The Apocryphal New Testament

(36) Jowett, George F., The Drama of the Lost Disciples, 1993

(37) Lewis, L. Smithett, The Holy Land of Britain

(38) Lipsius, R.A., Die apokryphen Apostelgeschichten und Apostellegenden, 2 vols., 1883. suppliement 1890

(39) Los Evangelios apocrifos (BAC 148), 1984, 1988

(40) The Lost Books of the Bible, 1926

(41) Mack, B. L., The Lost Gospel: The book of Q and Christian Origins, 1993

(42) Martin McNamara, The Apocrypha in the Irish Church, Dublin 1975

(43) Michaelis, Die Apocryphen Schriften zum Neuen Testament, Ubers. Und eri., 1958

(44) Migne, J. P., Patrologiae cursus completus., Series Graeca

(45) Montefiori, C., The Synoptic Gospels I, 2nd rev. ed. 1927

(46) Moraldi, Luigi, Apocrifi del nuovo Testamento, 2 vols., Apokryphe 1971

(47) Morgan, Rev. R. W, St. Paul in Britain

(48) Nag Hammadi Codex

(49) Nag Hammadi Studies

(50) Pagels, Elaine, The Gnostic Gospels, 1979

(51) Patrologia Orientalis, Paris

(52) Patristische Teste und Studien, 1964ff.

(53) Prydain, Genealogies of the Saints in Britain

(54) Rash A.F., This Sceptred Isle

(55) Riesner, R., and Betz, O., Jesus, Qumran and the Vatican, London 1994

(56) Rig-Vedas

(57) Robinson, James M., The Nag Hammadi Library in English, ed., Leiden 1977 (3rd revised ed. 1988)

(58) Ross, The History of England

(59) Sattin, A., Lifting the Veil: British Society in Egypt 1768-1956, London 1988

(60) Schneemelcher, Wilhelm, New Testament Apocrypha, vol 1-2

(61) Stanton, G., Gospel Truth? New Light on Jesus and the Gospels, 1995

(62) Thiede, C. P., Papyrus Magdalen

(63) Tischendorf, C., Apocalypses Apocryphae, ed. 1866

(64) Tischendorf, C., Evangelia Apocrypha, ed. C., 1876

(65) Vielhauer, Philip, Geschichte der ur christlichen Literatur, 1975

(66) Vishnu Purana

(67) Studies in New Testament and Early Christian Literature. Essays in Honour of Allen P. Wikgren, ed. E. E. Aune (Leiden, 1972)

POSTSCRIPT

There is a second wind in being able to see, and courage awaiting those who look again, and peace for those who see completely. Nature has its own way of compensating for the imperfection of our vision. Strangely, it is our acceptance of what we see within ourselves that grants us the power to be different.

He is the One who said come to me as little children. They are the ones who see pleasure amidst life's beautifully complex impurities. Those very impurities are what hide his footprints from sight so completely.

Glenn Kimball